Walking with Angels

By the same author

Spirited
Embracing Eternity
The Psychic Case Files

Walking with Angels

Tony Stockwell

HODDER &
STOUGHTON

First published in Great Britain in 2010 by Hodder & Stoughton
An Hachette UK company

3

Copyright © Tony Stockwell, 2010

The right of Tony Stockwell to be identified as the Author of the Work has been
asserted by him in accordance with the Copyright, Designs and Patents Act 1988.

A CIP catalogue record for this title is available from the British Library.

Trade Paperback ISBN 9 781 4447 0027 5

Typeset in Sabon by Hewer Text UK Ltd, Edinburgh
Printed and bound by CPI Mackays, Chatham ME5 8TD

Hodder & Stoughton policy is to use papers that are natural, renew-
able and recyclable products and made from wood grown in sustainable
forests. The logging and manufacturing processes are expected to conform
to the environmental regulations of the country of origin.

Hodder & Stoughton Ltd
338 Euston Road
London NW1 3BH

www.hodder.co.uk

I would like to dedicate this book to my adorable niece 'Princess' Evie, our little Angel here on earth. You bring such joy to those that love you, and may happiness follow you wherever you go.

Uncle Tony

Acknowledgements

My heartfelt thanks go to Stuart for his help and support, and for sharing this journey with me. Also to Lindsey, you are a star!

Contents

1. In the Beginning There Was Light   1

2. Journey to the Other Side   25

3. Onwards and Upwards   51

4. Miracles, Wonders and Signs   69

5. Superstars in the Sky   91

6. Twinkle, Twinkle, Little Stars   117

7. Healing with Angels   141

8. A Journey Quest   167

9. Bringing Spirit Into Your Life   185

10. A Lighter, Brighter You   203

I

In the Beginning There Was Light

'There are no strangers here; only friends you haven't yet met.'

William Butler Yeats

Even though I didn't want to accept it, on that memorable night not so long ago, I knew deep down that his fight for life was coming to a close. Now, as I listened to the gentle music and breathed in the fragrance of lilies in the candlelit room, I couldn't help but feel overcome by a sense of profound loss. I gazed at the items surrounding me: an arrangement of soft toys, a rugby shirt signed by the England team, a photograph showing Adam in happier times. And then I looked down at his coffin, thinking of the handsome, happy-go-lucky boy I had known, who had suffered so much during his brief stay here in this world and yet brought such warmth and joy to everyone who knew him.

I closed my eyes and sensed a presence next to me – no longer the boy in the wheelchair, but Adam, standing proud and upright beside me. Even though I was incredibly sad, I smiled to myself because I knew he was now free from his ravaged young body and happily reunited with his spirit family in the other world.

Just thirteen years old when he was taken from us, Adam had suffered oxygen deprivation at birth and battled against severe health problems all his life; but he had nonetheless confounded the expectations of the medical profession by surviving as long as he did – and with such a quality of life at that. Ultimately, his ailing body could cope no more, and a short time ago his mum, Karen, who was a close friend of mine, asked me to join her at the hospice in Guildford, Surrey, where Adam was being cared for.

We knew that night that any hope of improvement had ebbed away, and while Karen stepped out of the room to speak to the nurses, I sat with Adam and waffled on about rugby union, despite the fact that my knowledge of the sport was less than zero. But this had always been a joke between us and I endlessly wound Adam up with talk of, say, Ronnie Wilkinson's achievements in the England team's latest match. It drove him mad that I never got any of the players' names right and I have to confess that I did it again now, hoping that even though he couldn't respond he might at least be able to hear me and take with him the memory of the fun we used to have together.

A few moments later, I felt the familiar sensation that I associate with my spirit guide, Zintar, as he comes close to me. And then I heard his voice, speaking clearly into my mind, 'He's coming home soon. We're waiting for him to join us.'

I became aware that the room was filling with the most extraordinary energy; it felt as though the other world was trying to merge with this one – and perhaps that is what happens when somebody is preparing to pass from one to the other. This in itself was an incredible sensation, but then something powerful and beautiful happened that turned this moment into one I will never forget. As I stood there looking at Adam, thinking about how devastated his loving family would be when his time came to pass, he smiled up at me, as if to acknowledge my thoughts.

At first I felt it must be my imagination, but the presence of Zintar, along with an overpowering feeling of joy and serenity in the room, told me that anything was possible. Then, as I gazed towards the bed, Adam slowly rose up, sitting taller and straighter than I had ever seen him before, with a beaming smile that lit up the room. In the seconds that followed, which seemed like hours, I realised that the boy I was now seeing was free from all discomfort and the restrictions of his physical body; this was the spirit of Adam, no longer an ailing thirteen-year-old, but a healthy, vibrant spirit being – glorious, luminous and whole. The emotions emanating from him as our eyes met seemed to be both happiness that his trials here would soon be over and sadness that he would be physically leaving everyone who loved him so much.

As I acknowledged this, my thoughts again turned to his mum, sister and brothers, who would be so lost without him. As if picking up on these concerns, Adam's spirit voice came to me, saying, 'Look after them for me, Tony.' With that his spirit laid back down to join with his physical body on the bed. I sat there, motionless, trying to make sense of what had just happened, and I knew I had been privileged enough to have glimpsed the true, perfect essence of such an amazing boy.

After some time I bent closer to him and said softly, 'It's all right, you know, Adam. Everything's going to be fine. We'll all take care of your mum. You don't need to fight this any more.'

I remember Karen walking back into the room and sensing that something felt different. 'What's happening, Tony?

'The spirit people are here. They're just waiting for him to let go.'

Karen acknowledged this with the smallest nod; there was no need for further words between us.

Sometimes being a medium and feeling such things as I did in Adam's room that night is difficult; but that's just how it's always been for me. Ever since I can remember, I've known things before they have happened, I've seen the spirits of the departed and I've learned over many years how to listen to them and pass on their messages to those they have left behind. This hasn't always been easy, but I still view it as the greatest blessing in my life; and now, thanks to this gift and all the experiences it brings, when I think of Adam I know that he is walking with the angels.

It still sometimes seems strange even to me that I should have been singled out to lead a life filled with such extraordinary experiences, especially when I think of my unremarkable origins. I was born on 20 February 1969 in the ordinary suburb of Walthamstow, east London. For reasons entirely unassociated with that event, it was a good year: Concorde soared into its maiden supersonic flight and Neil Armstrong made a giant leap for mankind as he took those momentous first steps on the moon.

My first steps were obviously some way off at that point, and apparently I wasn't interested in doing very much at all – I was a huge, fat, contented baby who slept constantly and woke only at feeding times. I guess I must have known right from the start how much I was loved.

I may have been new and bouncing, but it's my strong belief that the soul that blended with my little body as it started its life journey was perhaps as old as mankind itself. As readers of my previous books will know, I believe that my spirit has been through many different lifetimes on this Earth, returning to the spirit world each time the human body dies and coming back at an indeterminate future point in another body, to learn, grow and evolve. In other words, I've been round the block a few times!

So have you all, if you did but know it. I recognise that many of you may not as yet have been fortunate enough to glimpse the world I'm speaking about, but I sincerely hope that in journeying with me through the pages of this book you will open your hearts and minds to the experiences, feelings and beliefs I describe. One of my favourite quotations came from the brilliant mind of George Bernard Shaw: '*Some men see things as they are and ask why. Others dream things that never were and ask why not.*' It will probably come as little surprise to you when I say that I personally think the 'why not' school of thought is much more fun. One or two of you, I've no doubt, will be thinking, 'This guy should be carted off by the men in white coats,' but with any luck the rest of you will be saying, 'OK, let's just see where this thing leads. Where are we off to now then, Tony?'

We're off to the house where I spent the first four years of my life: a high-ceilinged, Victorian terrace with three good-sized bedrooms – the kind of house that would probably fetch a small fortune today, but forty years ago was considered quite ordinary and humble. My dad was a painter and decorator and my mum, at that time, a hairdresser. They were not wealthy, far from it in fact, but worked hard and were always able to provide for my older sister Lorraine and me, even if it meant missing out on things for themselves. Little did they suspect at that time how their only son would end up following a rather more unusual line of work than their own.

For me, work is not a career but a life path. I don't see how I could have worked as anything other than a medium. I'm a very ordinary guy, but blessed with an extraordinary gift, one that as I'm sure you can imagine is quite difficult to ignore – rather like those young witches and wizards so eager to attend that school of wizardry in the famous books of J.K. Rowling. I was hardly going to say to a careers officer at school, 'Well, what I really want is to be a postman, only these dead people keep telling me they have something else in mind.' So my fate was sealed, and for the last twenty years I have been privileged to work as a medium, having started out at the age of nineteen.

Even as a very small child, aged only four, I was aware of the spirit world, although I wouldn't have recognised it then for was what it actually was. My bedtime ritual started out much the same as any other child's, with bath time. My mother would pop me into the old plastic bath that sat incongruously alongside the rather divine turquoise hand-basin and chain-flush loo, and attempt to run a sponge over me as I splashed around, determinedly trying to sink a large plastic boat with a fleet of ill-disciplined rubber ducks. I vividly recall the huge, soft towel Mum would wrap me in afterwards, followed by a light dusting of talc and the cool feel of crisp, clean pyjamas.

Believing I was like most other children and reluctant to settle down to sleep, Mum would then lovingly regale me with nursery rhymes and fairy tales, blissfully unaware that I couldn't wait for her stories to end and the real adventures to begin. Only after she kissed my forehead, murmured her customary, 'Night night, Fruitgum' (no, I don't know where that came from either!) and then turned off the light and shut the door softly behind her was I free to start a new adventure – not here, but away in a land of joyous faces, unparalleled colour and music of indescribable beauty.

I sat in my bed, wide-eyed, staring out into a sea of nothingness, waiting for the vision to arrive. When it did it was incredibly clear, starting with a pinprick of light in the corner of the room and growing bigger, brighter and always highly coloured, sometimes swirling, like a vortex between this world and the next. It's difficult to describe, but as the light grew, the smiling faces materialised – perhaps a woman with long, blonde hair, neatly braided, or a man with an ebony complexion and eyes as dark as coal, but seemed to light up as he smiled. It was as though they were speaking to me without words, calling my name, though I didn't hear them. Their messages resonated deep in the core of me, always kind, always simple. 'Can he hear us?' 'Yes, I think he can!' No matter how differently they appeared, I knew they were somehow related, all of one family, yet not as I knew my everyday family. Looking back, some of the visions of my childhood came to me so easily that they were clearer then than at any other time of my mediumistic life.

On occasion, a special visitor would come – a young woman of around twenty, her hair in ringlets, skin white as milk, eyes as brilliant green as the finest emeralds. She seemed to enter the room through the bright, swirling light and would stand over my bed as solid as any person I might see about me in real life. She would lean forward and tend to me, almost as though she was my mum – I thought she must have been someone's mum, despite her youth. I somehow knew that she wasn't alive, but this didn't trouble me. I began to think of her in my mind as my mum who visited me in the night – or 'the soft lady', such was the comfort of her presence. Sometimes she would sing to me, words I can no longer recall, tunes that have long since left me. But I can remember how the song she sang made me feel warm, complete and safe as my tired eyes gradually closed.

I've always thought of sleep as a great healer, soothing the mind, resting the body and sometimes bringing a whole new perspective to our lives. I guess that's why people often say, 'Let's sleep on it,' or, 'You'll feel better in the morning.' Since those early childhood adventures in the playground of sleep, I have come to believe that during our nightly slumbers the spirit part of us is able to journey from our bodies and enter the spirit kingdom. While there, we might see and experience things that enrich our soul, although for many people the memories of these experiences fall away as we awaken and re-enter the physical reality governed by the conscious mind. So just for a moment consider that each night when you go to sleep, it might be that while your body rests this is also a time when your spirit soars and is set free. Going back to the words of George Bernard Shaw, 'Why not?'

Perhaps I could so vividly remember my experiences during sleep at this time because I was of such a tender age. As a four-year-old, I'd only been away from my true home for four years. I now believe that the longer we live, the harder it is for us to remember where we have really come from, that our true home is in fact the spirit world. For someone who has experienced the reality of their own eternal spirit during childhood it is one of the greatest possible achievements to retain and maintain these memories. For those who have forgotten the true inheritance of their soul and what they are here to achieve, today may be the first day on which they can start to remember.

I never felt scared during my night-time experiences as a child. As my eyes became heavy and sleep enfolded me, I frequently felt myself falling backwards, but far from resisting this precarious sensation I always went with it, wanting to see where I would land. I have a vivid recollection of often floating above my own body, seeing myself fast asleep – like a modern-day cherub. I would look down at this warm, podgy, smooth-skinned body with sun-bleached hair and feel a deep sense of contentment. Reflecting now, I believe that my spirit within was satisfied that I would one day grow up to recognise my mission and help and hopefully inspire other people. But at the time, I only knew that the little body I looked down on was just a small part of me and that the greater part was about to have an amazing experience.

It would begin with the sense that I was travelling at great speed, the wind in my face, surrounded by dazzling white light as I became aware of a land of adventure in the near distance.

On one such occasion, I found myself sitting on the steps of some kind of church, mosque or synagogue. I wasn't exactly sure what it was, but I knew it was a place devoted to communion with God, or the Great Spirit. For some reason I made no attempt to enter, as though I was only allowed to go as far as the steps. I then became aware of a figure appearing; even all these years later, I clearly remember it was a young person, with fair hair and tanned skin, barefoot and casually dressed in an open-necked shirt and light-coloured trousers. To begin with, I wasn't sure whether it was a man or a woman – there was an androgynous quality to the appearance – but I knew it was a man when I heard him speak. He introduced himself and while I struggle to remember his exact words, I knew he was imparting important information, teaching me, and that I should pay close attention to the messages he brought.

There were many subsequent encounters where my new friend would bring further lessons, gifts to my spirit that would in later life be invaluable to the work I needed to carry out. He told me that the journey my life would take was not like that of most boys and girls: I was here for a different purpose and he had great hopes for me.

I wouldn't want to suggest that this spirit man was God – in fact I'm sure he wasn't – but there did seem to be a spark of the divine about him and I believe that the feeling I had in his presence might just begin to suggest how it might feel to look into the face of God. I felt a love so unconditional and so powerful that these early experiences changed my life forever.

I now know this joyful soul from the other world is called Peter and he sometimes draws close to assist me in my work.

I think of him as a guardian and a teacher, an individual utterly uncomplicated and unlimited by the emotions and needs of the physical world. He appears to me as someone who seems to hold all the knowledge of the universe within him – a messenger of God, an angelic being.

I am sure that on reading this, my fourth book, even some of my closest friends might be a little shocked to discover that I have for many years been journeying to the other world in this way. But it is only now that I feel confident and free enough to share with them and with you my full spirit experience and the visions and information I have been privileged to be given from the higher world. I know that some of what I say will seem far-fetched and other things too good to believe, but I can tell you now that these are my experiences. All that I share with you is my reality and it has brought me great happiness and fulfilment. I hope it will have a similar effect for you.

Let me ask you to do something. As you hold this book in your hands, consider your body, whether you are comfortable where you sit, how your back, neck and shoulders feel. Be aware of the rhythm of your breathing and just for a moment tune into the sounds and smells that surround you, recognising that all these sensations are of the physical world and the physical body we inhabit. Now, become conscious of how you feel as you read these words, of how you are no doubt asking questions as you read, and then acknowledge that what you are experiencing while reading is processed by the brain and is therefore by its very nature limited, since our brains contain only the memories of our Earthly lives and nothing of our experiences before birth.

The next step is difficult. Try to imagine that you are no longer limited by a physical body and brain, and then endeavour to let go of all your emotional hang-ups, phobias and desires – in fact all of the memories of the experiences that have shaped your life to this moment. Then ask yourself, 'Without these things, and besides my physical body, what am I, who am I?'

For some of you the answer will be nothing. But for others there might be a surge of excitement as you acknowledge the existence of a greater part of your self. Try to believe me when I tell you that you are a spirit being, from another world but now here in the physical world. For you to dwell here, you need a body to anchor yourself into this reality, and the brain is a precious part of that body, allowing you to speak and move, get from A to B and live a full and expressive physical life. But beyond all of this, we are eternal beings, intrinsically linked, making up part of the whole, that 'whole' being a universal consciousness.

You might naturally then wish to ask, 'If I am this spirit being, why am I here? What is the point of it all?' The answer lies within each one of us, but is, I believe, similar for all: to triumph over adversity, to bring light where there is darkness, love where there is hate, healing where there is pain and laughter where there is sadness – to grow and be an expression of all we can be. When we bring beauty into the world, it is a reflection of our heart's desire and comes from our spirit within.

If you are anything like me, the thought that there is no end and no beginning, that there has never been a moment when we have not existed is enough to make your head spin. But I still believe it to be true. I have never felt the need to follow one particular religious faith and tend to cherry-pick the parts of each that appeal the most. I have, however, found many of the answers I sought in Spiritualism – its simplicity and absolute belief in communication with the spirit world resonates with me completely.

A quotation I am particularly fond of, though sadly I can't recall its origin, sums up my philosophy nicely: '*Let go of religion and embrace God.*' When I talk of God, broadly I am thinking of the ultimate force that breathes life into all beings, the eternal energy of the universe. Since the beginning of time, men and women have pondered the meaning of life and many religions and philosophies have been born from the need to try and make sense of our existence. I strongly believe that the answers do not lie solely within books and the teachings of others, but that all we need to know lies within us. Each of us is linked to a powerful force – one that will continue to grow as we do – and the life we live now is a very small chapter in the story of our eternal lives.

I believe, without exception, that we come into the world with good intent and the desire to bring blessings into our environments. But of course not everyone is able to see this through. For some, such as those born into abusive homes, whose life experience is harsh from the earliest stages, the emotional scars can be so deep that it is very difficult for their souls to express themselves. Others might develop physical or mental problems that act as an obstacle to the spirit's true expression.

We all know that bad things happen while we're here in the world – we only need to turn on the radio or TV to find murder, mayhem and mischief occurring constantly around the globe. But I believe that the answer to the age-old question, 'If there is a God, why do such bad things happen?' is that people act in destructive and violent ways because they are detached from their own spirit and not listening to the true voice within them. They have not recognised that they are made up of so much more than emotions, a brain and a physical body. If each of us had an epiphany, realising that we are a spirit of divine love and accepting the consequences of our own actions, I wonder how different the world might be.

We hold the secrets of the universe within us. I hope to explain, from my own soul's perspective, how the spirit world influences our lives, as well as show you who these spirit beings are and something of the hierarchy that exists within the realm beyond the veil we call death.

I believe each of us has a beautiful spirit being that has elected to be with us from the moment of our physical birth until the moment we pass. Before we're born, we might seek the help of one of our oldest friends, or guides, in the other world. Imagine a conversation that might go something like this:

> You: I'm thinking of going back to Earth for another go.
> Guide: Seriously? It's hard work down there.
> You: (with a wink) They need as much help as they can get.
> Guide: What d'you have in mind this time then?
> You: Music. I want to develop my love of music and hopefully do really well.
> Guide: You mean you want to be rich and famous.
> You: Riches may bring their own rewards. I'd like to set up an orphanage.
> Guide: Now you're talking. I'll do my best to help you to make that happen. (reflects a moment) Maybe we could get you on *The X Factor*.

OK, I'm having a little fun and that's all very simplistic, but it's just a way of saying that the role of our spirit guides is to advise us and help us achieve what we set out to do for ourselves.

Our guides, like ourselves, are individual spirit beings with a host of experiences gained both from lives lived here in the physical world and those lived in the spirit world. They walk and they communicate with each other just as we do while we're here. But they have reached a greater level of spiritual attunement, a higher sense of awareness as to who they are and what they will achieve in the future. They are the sum total of all their experiences and therefore in a wonderful position to teach and inspire us, and to be our confidants and counsellors. They might come to us in the form of Native American Indians, venerable Chinamen or gracious Japanese ladies, and perhaps they create such distinctive guises for themselves so that we will recognise and know them – although they could just as easily look like a man in a business suit or a woman from the school run.

When my own guide, Zintar, first appeared to me, he showed himself as a very old and wise Tibetan monk, with flowing saffron robes, sandals on his feet, a bald head and a wizened look, all of which evoked within me a deep sense of respect for him and his age-old knowledge. Over the years, as our relationship has grown, I've come to accept him completely as my guide, but each time he draws near I greet him more and more as a friend. No longer does he feel the need to show himself as he did that first time; in fact, the more I think about it, he often chooses not to show himself at all. Instead, I become aware of the gentle influence of a wise man from the other world gathering close.

During the years I've worked as a medium, I've heard people request of their guides the most unusual things, ranging from a car park space to a lottery win. Now, even if they were privy to that kind of information, I'm sure our guides have better things to do than help us at this level! We should respect and appreciate the huge efforts they make on our behalf; they support us when we're down, bring inspiration when it's needed, are there to talk to as we would a dear friend and are hopeful that we will recognise them while we are here in the world – and in so doing continue a loving relationship with them.

Sometimes our guides show themselves to us in a dramatic way to remind us of the experiences we've shared with them in a past lifetime. So a guide who chooses to reveal himself as a Mongolian warrior, with a yak skin upon his back and laden with weapons, might well be prompting you to remember a life once lived in the bleak landscape of the Gobi desert. Each time he comes through, and as the relationship grows, as with Zintar, he might feel less and less the need to show himself in such a dramatic fashion.

As we open our minds to embrace our soul's previous experiences, a number of spirit guides might visit us, although not all of them will remain with us. There was a period when I became quite confused about the whole subject of guides and guardian spirits. During the past twenty odd years I've been to many one-to-one sittings with other mediums, and they were convinced that the guide they described to me, complete with name and personality, was my number one guardian spirit – the one who would guide me through the rest of my life. I've been given an African warrior, a Native American Indian and a Benedictine nun – goodness only knows what she thought of me! – and yet I have never heard from them again.

One such reading was notable for all the wrong reasons. I must have been about twenty-two at the time and working in east London's Docklands, in the finance department of a Danish shipping company. It was a fantastic company to work for, but they certainly required their pound of flesh, often expecting us to work late into the evening. On the final day of the month-end accounts, it was past three o'clock in the afternoon and I still had plenty of work to do. But all I

could think about was that I had to be out the door by five
o'clock sharp if I was to make it to an appointment I had long
been looking forward to: I was due to visit a very elderly and
highly respected medium.

Each time I looked at the clock, it was as if someone had
purposely wound it forward at double speed; I was running
out of time fast. Working next to me was Sade, a beautiful
young girl, originally from Nigeria, with whom I'd struck up
a friendship. We often talked about the nature of human-
ity and spirituality, although I must confess that every time I
spoke to her about the spirit world she glazed over uncom-
prehendingly. When I glanced across at her, she picked up an
air of desperation.

'Have you lost the company millions again?' she quipped.

'Worse,' I replied. 'If I don't get out of here in the next ten
minutes, I'm going to miss my appointment.'

'What, with the doctor? I thought you looked a bit peaky.'

'Oh, thanks,' I bristled. 'I'm fine.' Then, feeling slightly
sheepish, I added, 'Actually it's with a clairvoyant. She's
supposed to be really good.'

Sade snorted. 'Then she'll know you're running late, won't
she?' Catching my expression, she added briskly, 'Just ring
and reschedule. We've got tons to do here.'

I knew that was the only sensible thing to do, but I wasn't
feeling particularly sensible at that moment and couldn't help
muttering, 'Sure, no problem, I've only waited six months to
see her.'

I could feel my face turning bright red so I buried my head
in my papers again and tried to get on with some work. A
few moments later, a slender, gentle hand came to rest on
mine.

'Just tell me what needs to be done and I'll finish up,' said
Sade.

I left on the dot of five that evening and even now, all these years later, I remember how that simple act of kindness made me feel. But little did I know how my evening was going to pan out.

A couple of hours later, freshly bathed, with a clean white shirt and smelling a little too strongly of Kouros – definitely an acquired taste in men's fragrance – I found myself opening a creaky and rusty wrought iron gate. There was a large black cat sat directly in the middle of the narrow garden path, eyeing me with disdain and refusing to budge, so I had to step onto the flowerbed to move around it. As I looked into his face, I saw that one eye was missing, his tongue seemed to flop out from one side of his mouth and much of one ear had probably gone the same way as the absent eye. The poor creature looked like something from another world and I began to get a strange feeling about what lay ahead.

I must admit I was already a little nervous as I'd heard that the old lady, although gifted, was rather eccentric and perhaps a little batty to boot. But mindful of Sade's sacrifice – and that she was no doubt still grafting away in the office – I took a deep breath and rang the bell.

The door was flung open immediately, almost as though the medium had been lying in wait. 'Enter,' she said, with a theatrical flourish that reminded me of something out of a horror film. She led me through to her lounge, where a large, round, wooden table stood in the centre of the room. There were lit candles everywhere, some right next to the moth-eaten curtains, and the first thought that ran through my mind was that this house was a fire hazard. She ushered me to the table and asked me to sit. To be honest, I really wanted to use the bathroom, but as she'd already sat down opposite me and closed her eyes, I remained silent – believe it or not I was quite shy back then.

She was dressed plainly in a beige, hand-knitted cardigan, but heavily made up, with an evident passion for blue mascara. Her ample chest rose steadily as she started to inhale deeply. This went on for some time, then, with a start, she began to speak in a voice that was not her own. 'I am your guide,' she boomed. 'My name is Ramar. I have been waiting for this moment for a very long time. Welcome, my son.'

I sat there, open mouthed, uncertain whether to laugh or head for the hills, but sure in the knowledge that neither would be appropriate. As I listened over the course of the next hour, Ramar told me many things, none of which made any sense. He spoke to me of my life and its purpose, but again none of this seemed to resonate or touch me in the way I knew it would if this really was someone from the spirit world.

Towards the end of the consultation, I was asked, 'My son, do you have any questions?' And of course I did. I asked if my guide, Zintar, could come through, or whether he was aware of me in that moment. At this point the medium became flustered, but nothing could have prepared me for the fact that she then proceeded to tell me that Zintar did not exist.

Well, I'm not in the habit of telling lies or running down other mediums, but I promise you that as she lowered her head I spotted her sneaking a quick peek at her watch – whereupon she immediately came out of her 'trance' and demanded her £15 fee. Before I could gather my wits, I stupidly handed it to her.

Looking rather pleased with herself, she asked me what I thought of the message. As I said, I was quite shy at that age so I don't know where my reply came from, but I squared my shoulders and told her, 'The person coming through wasn't my guide. I think you might have got your spirit wires crossed.' She turned four shades of crimson and ushered me out the door.

I felt deflated and annoyed as I left the house. The cat was still sitting in the middle of the path and I swear he smiled as I did my little detour around him. I wonder now how often that cat has seen the same look of displeasure on a client's face as they left the house.

To cap it all, I learned the next day that poor Sade had been toiling away in the office on my behalf until well after midnight. I felt guilty and annoyed, which was not assisted by the fact that my wallet was now £15 lighter.

So for those of you who have an earnest desire to know who it is that looks after you from the other world, it might be easier and far more accurate to invite your guardian close to you directly. With a little practice, which we will touch on later, you will learn to recognise the subtle changes within your sensitivity as these enlightened beings draw near.

For those of us who truly wish to do good deeds for the benefit of others, whether in the line of mediumship, healing or anything else that makes a difference, there will be many from the other world who will take an interest in us. You may know them from previous experiences and it is up to you as an individual to sense who your guardian is. I believe there is always one spirit being we have forged a relationship with before we are born and it is this individual who has promised to lead, help and guide us successfully in our mission here on Earth. We should, of course, still remain open to the influences of other learned and gentle spirit beings who might gather close to us, and accept them as inspirers, teachers and friends.

So let's now consider the age-old questions, 'What are angels?', 'Do they really exist?' and 'Who is my angel?'

While many of us in modern western society assume that angels are associated with Christianity, references to their existence date back almost to the beginning of time. The word 'angel' is derived from the Ancient Greek word for messenger, 'angelos', and therefore dates back a few centuries before the birth of Christ. Going back several thousand years before that, there is evidence that winged spiritual beings were embraced by the practitioners of Shamanism in Central Asia in pre-Sumerian times. The religion of Zoroastrianism, founded by the prophet Zarathustra in Ancient Persia in around 1200 BC, comprised a structure of six main Archangels presiding over a tier of lesser angels known as 'the Adorable Ones'. Below them were the personal angels, believed to act as an individual's guide, protector and conscience.

Angels are referred to in the Islamic Koran as messengers 'with wings, two, three or four' and feature in the Jewish faith as a 'heavenly court' whose purpose is to communicate God's messages to His people. In Christianity, it was an angel who appeared to Joseph in a dream, telling him that the child in Mary's womb was divinely conceived; and Mary herself was told by the angel Gabriel that she had found favour with God and would conceive in her womb a son who would be called Jesus.

So, as you can appreciate, angels have long since played a part in our forebears' religious and spiritual beliefs. I recognise that for many of us in the western world, inhabiting as we do a space that seems consumed by materialism and technological advances, it is increasingly difficult to accept the concept of messengers of God wanting to play any part in our lives – lives stunted by money, possessions and position. But these advanced spirit beings have never before had a greater need to intercede and influence our lives for the better.

Angels are often described as winged beings, and there are many accounts of white feathers, thought by some to be from angels' wings, being found in places where it would seem inconceivable for them to appear. I recently heard of a woman who, full of despair and angst, asked for a sign that she was not alone and that God would hear her prayers. She found a pure white feather, at least eight inches long, directly under her pillow as she went to bed that evening. She took this as a sign that her prayers were indeed being heard.

In my experience, though feathers might be found, they are more a manifestation of the angels' intent rather than a calling card from their wings. When I see angelic beings, they are surrounded by, or emanate, a pure white glow that gives the impression of wings. I believe it is this powerful phenomenon that caused seers and sensitives to describe them as winged beings.

This might perplex some of you, especially if you've heard stories depicting these divine entities in the traditional form. But, rather like our first experiences with our own spirit guide, it's possible that the angels choose to show themselves in the traditional manner simply to convey their angelic status.

An example of this is a profound experience I had when I was thirteen, when my family was moving house. Our new home was full of boxes and my nan and auntie were busily unpacking, bleaching cupboards and scrubbing toilets so that we could settle in quickly. It was all hands to the deck, and our new home was buzzing with excitement, laughter and activity.

And then there was me. Rather than sorting out my new bedroom, I was curled up on my bed, grunting in agony. I had a temperature, I felt sick and my stomach hurt. So consumed were my family with the job at hand that my plight went unnoticed for some hours. By the time my mum discovered me, I didn't feel well at all. The rest of it is something of a blur. An ambulance was called and the next thing I knew I was in Southend-on-Sea Hospital. After a few preliminary checks, I was wrapped in a hospital gown, and with a sense of urgency wheeled down a long, echoey corridor. Unbeknown to me, I had acute appendicitis and needed emergency surgery. I remember waving a feeble goodbye to my mum and dad as the doors swung open to admit me to the operating theatre.

During the operation I found myself floating above my own body, watching as the surgeons carried out the procedure. I felt no fear, no angst or panic, but watched the whole thing as it unfolded before my eyes. Strangely, even at that age, I knew I was out of my body and it wasn't a dream. The experience felt intensely real.

I suddenly became aware of two bright lights, one either side of me – dazzling, effervescent, powerful. As I became more accustomed to them, I saw within each one a beautiful entity, on my right side a man and on my left a woman. Then I felt them take my hands and in a moment we were flying high, pulled at great speed by an invisible force. We left the hospital behind us and I was aware that I had also left my physical body behind. Then with a jolt I found myself in a place I can only describe as heavenly, and I knew instinctively that this woman and man were angels. I saw no wings and yet we soared like birds. I remember being dazzled by their light, but what will stay with me more than anything else is how these spirit beings made me feel. They seemed to know me, inside and out, and there was no need for them to speak to me because I received their messages telepathically as their minds blended with mine.

Their words flowed effortlessly into my thoughts, clearly and simply: 'All will be well, we are here to heal you and make you better. You have been born for a reason, you have been born with a purpose and you will not return to us just yet.' It then felt as though their thoughts were being directed throughout my body and I was bathed in dazzling colour that filled my entire body.

With the passage of time, I can't remember all the details of this experience, but I can honestly say I know how it feels to be in the presence of angels.

Perhaps the full memory of the experience was erased almost immediately, because if I'd held within me all the wonderful feelings inspired by this place, it might have deterred me from returning to the physical world to accomplish my life's goals. What remains with me most vividly is a revelation spoken without words: that each of us is a part of the whole, the whole being God, the divine power, and each of us is directly connected to this loving force. Whether we are in this world or in the spiritual world, it makes little difference: we are all united and connected, you and I are the same. When we follow the path of enlightenment, we are led to the simple realisation that we are a part of God and because of that, unlimited in our possibilities for happiness. We are here to exude and to receive love, from both sides of life.

2

Journey to the Other Side

'When I died, I saw angels. Beautiful and bright. They
smiled at me and made me feel so at home.'

The spirit of Malcolm

As you will have gathered, it is my strong belief that each
of us is a spirit person having a physical experience here on
Earth. Our spirit knows that our time here is both precious
and limited and remains in constant connection with our
spiritual home. The essence of this was illustrated to me not
so very long ago through a vivid and powerful vision.

While in deep meditation, I was shown our world and the
millions and millions of people who inhabit this space we
call Earth. I became conscious of how each was completely
consumed in their own lives, their own wants and needs. I
then felt the spiritual aspect of all these human beings, but
what struck me most was that each of them had an ethereal
silver thread emanating from the head and running upwards
into the sky. As soon as I saw this, I realised these 'cords' of
silver energy were linked to the spirit of us, holding us and
maintaining a constant flow of awareness and connection
with the Great Spirit, or God. It was indescribably reassuring
to recognise that every one of us is constantly linked to the
power that is unconditional love. Even those who we describe
as 'sleepwalking' during their time on Earth – people who
never see the beauty of creation or appreciate loving relationships and the joy that can be gained from the simplest

of pursuits – even they are linked to the divine and adored as powerfully as those who have already attained a level of enlightenment or understanding.

I was left with the deeply comforting feeling that, even in our darkest moments – moments of danger, despair, violence or tragedy – we are still linked and bound together. It seems to me that much of the purpose of life is to strive to reach a level of recognition, understanding and acceptance that we are eternal beings.

We have only to look about us – at world issues, those who fight each other for no reason other than religious intolerance, racial prejudice or simply for being different – to see that it must be quite difficult for the spirit people, our guides and angels, to comprehend why we should look for the differences in each other rather than the similarities. A bereft mother in Beirut shares the same grief as a bereft mother from Islington. The joy of a proud father as he gazes at his newborn child in a high-rise block of flats in Glasgow is similar to the pride of a new father in a village in Ethiopia. Cultures may differ but the fundamental emotions that rule us are the same. It may seem trite to say, but how much brighter and happier would our experiences of this world be if we were to let go of all prejudices, whether inherited or brought about by social and economic factors. Imagine the freedom we would find to love our fellow human beings the world over, regardless of how they look or the language they speak; it is the freedom of recognising that we are all brothers and sisters under the skin.

This will ring especially true for those of you who already accept the concept of reincarnation, for you know you have experienced numerous lives, with many shades of skin colour and diverse languages and cultures, each one contributing to the vast tapestry of your spirit's existence.

When I was about nine years old and still at junior school, my teacher Mrs Martin took the class one Easter to the Church of England church across the road from the school. I remember being really excited, because I knew I was going into 'God's House'. I'm not sure quite where this enthusiasm came from because I had never been to any kind of church with my parents and religious education wasn't part of my upbringing. I remember my mum telling me that I was Church of England, but with hindsight I'm sure this was only an insurance policy in case I was ever knocked down by a car!

On entering the church, I was immediately struck by the coolness of the air and the slightly musty smell of old hymn books. We were lucky that the organist was playing and I loved the sound of his music, together with the sense of peace that pervaded this sacred place.

As we settled ourselves among the pews, the vicar addressed us, speaking of Jesus' miracles and the love he had for each of us. But as this went on, I found myself fighting to hold back a veil of tiredness. You will not be surprised to learn that I failed miserably.

All thoughts of Jesus and Easter left me but, strangely, although it seemed I'd fallen asleep, I was still aware of the hardness of the cold wooden seat and the fidgeting and occasional sniggering of the children around me. Despite this, it felt as though the walls of the church and the church itself were somehow a thousand miles away. I could hear the sounds of people chanting and gongs being struck; the air was suffused with the heady aroma of incense and my thoughts were now completely consumed by the vision and the name of Buddha. At that age, my experience of such a thing must surely have been limited to some vague reference from an old movie; yet it felt so real at that moment that I somehow knew I was closer to what I thought of as heaven than I had ever been in my life. Here I was, a pasty-faced, blonde-haired kid from a working-class background in Essex, with next to no religious conviction, suddenly experiencing the sights, colours, scents and sounds of a Buddhist temple! So real and intense were my feelings that I truly believed I was there.

As though enveloped in love, it all felt so incredible that my emotions got the better of me. I felt myself begin to cry, and then soon the trickle became a torrent as the first few tears gave way to all-out sobbing, almost to the point of wailing. Perhaps not surprisingly, I suddenly felt the tight grip of Mrs Martin's hand around my arm. She hauled me unceremoniously from my seat, and as she did the spell was broken and I came tumbling back to reality – a reality where a vicar and seemingly a thousand children were staring in disbelief at this puffy-eyed, weird kid. As Mrs Martin escorted me briskly from the church and out into the open air, I tried to explain to her the incredible feelings I had experienced, but it all fell on deaf ears. I was marched back to school and ordered to reflect on my 'appalling outburst'. I just couldn't understand how an experience so unbelievably wonderful could have led to my being installed on a rickety chair in the 'naughty corner'.

As I sat there, feeling very sorry for myself, words my grandmother had so often spoken when reflecting on my actions came back to haunt me: 'God he's weird.' She would sometimes qualify this with, 'He's a lovely boy but so different from the rest of them,' and now I wondered whether she was right and if I would ever fit in with the others at school. But as I pondered, it seemed that being strange or different wasn't such a bad thing. If my school friends had just closed their eyes and allowed it to happen, they might have had the same loving experience as I had.

Looking back all these years later, it seems that there are key moments in our lives when we are receptive to the guidance of the spirit people. If we unwittingly allow these moments to pass us by, or worse still ignore them, we could miss out on so much that it could be detrimental to our lives. It's not all about being psychic or mediumistic, or receiving visions and voices, it's more about being open to inspiration – spiritual experiences are there for everyone. Even as adults, finding ourselves saddled with mortgages, pressures and responsibilities, we can't just plod on waiting for life to happen, hoping that we will have the necessary finances and emotional reserves to deal with all that life throws at us. It's never too late to understand that we too are very much a part of the creative force and that life is what we make it. Then we can open ourselves at will to be inspired, nurtured and healed – and in so doing embrace our lives, both in this world and the next.

There's a quote I love from J.M. Barrie's *Peter Pan*: 'To die will be an awfully big adventure.' Wouldn't it be wonderful if we could share this philosophy! We all know that, as sure as we are born, one day we will die. For each of us there will come a point when we take our last breath, our heart will no longer beat and our bodies will cease to function. Just imagine how that might be, and rather than feel a sense of sadness or fear, embrace the idea that this is not the end but the start of something new and wondrous – just as when Peter Pan, at the helm of Captain Hook's ship, headed off for new adventures after returning Wendy and the boys home to London.

The moment our physical bodies cease to function, the spirit part of us is automatically released, the link between body and spirit severed. Then the silver cord I previously mentioned – the thread that links us to the divine – pulls us gently and effortlessly homewards, back to the spirit world.

There are thousands of written testimonies of this journey – by people who had near-death experiences. They describe how they believe that they actually passed over and journeyed to the spirit world, or heaven, only to be resuscitated here in the physical world so that their spirit reunited with their body.

Several years ago, I was invited to tour a number of venues on both islands of New Zealand. I arrived in South Island's Dunedin, massively jet-lagged but thankfully there was a one-day break before the tour began in earnest.

While in Dunedin, I met a very bubbly woman of about my age, whose name was Carol. She spotted me in the foyer of the hotel where I was staying and came running towards me, having recognised my face from the numerous posters pinned up around the town. She shook me rather too energetically by the hand, speaking nineteen to the dozen, and at first I struggled to grasp what she was saying. Her appearance was dishevelled, to put it politely, and she came across as slightly bonkers, so I did my best to keep the conversation short. As I turned to leave, she called after me, 'I'll see you tomorrow at your demonstration. Really looking forward to it.'

'Oh well,' I thought, 'she's enthusiastic if nothing else.'

After the demonstration the next evening, I wandered back to the hotel. On entering the foyer, a woman came up to me with a big smile and it was only when she spoke that I recognised her as Carol. Without meaning any disrespect, she looked as though she'd had a major makeover. As if she'd read my thoughts, she said, 'I can turn into a butterfly when I want, you know.' And as I looked at her, that's exactly what she reminded me of – something lively, full of colour and free-spirited.

Carol spent a couple of minutes raving about the demonstration and telling me she was my greatest fan. Well, what could I do but ask if she would like to join me for a drink in the hotel bar.

As it turned out, we got along famously. She was bright and funny, although perhaps still a little bonkers because she thought I was funny too. We spoke of many things – New Zealand's stunning landscapes, fabulous food and different pace of life – and eventually the conversation turned to the subject of the spirit world, mediumship and all things psychic-related.

Carol bombarded me with a whole host of questions, from the subject of haunted houses to what happens when a pet passes to the spirit world, and I did my best to answer as fully and sincerely as I could. She then asked what I thought about near-death experiences and I shared with her my own adventures in this respect. Sensing quite strongly that she herself had had a similar experience, I asked why she had such an avid interest in this phenomenon. She grinned back at me and said, 'I think I might need another drink before that one.'

A few minutes later, while nursing a replenished glass of New Zealand Sauvignon Blanc, Carol began her story, prefacing it with, 'I'm not a religious person at all and I didn't really believe in anything spiritual beforehand. But anyway, here's what happened.'

Years before, when she was in her late teens, Carol had taken her father's Jeep to visit some friends who lived a few miles away. Even though still only a young woman, she had been driving for years, having first learned on her parents' farm, and she considered herself very accomplished behind the wheel.

It was already dark by the time she left home that night and it had been raining hard for several days. The weather showed no sign of letting up, but she was anxious to see her friends and so set out regardless. When she was a short distance from her friends' home, travelling down a narrow country road, the rain pounding on her windscreen, a large lorry suddenly came hurtling round a bend towards her. In a desperate attempt to avoid a collision she instinctively turned the steering wheel hard and veered off the road. Little was she to know that she was turning into a deep gorge and felt the Jeep lurch as the ground disappeared from beneath it. Then she recalled the vehicle bouncing into trees and rocks and flipping over several times as it plummeted into the ravine.

'The next thing I knew,' she said, 'I was standing outside the Jeep. It had landed upside down on some jagged rocks and steam and smoke were billowing everywhere. I looked at myself, at my hands and my legs, then felt my face and my head, but I seemed to be completely unhurt.'

Carol was amazed. Even her clothes were without a mark and despite her terrifying ordeal she felt totally lucid, though she had no memory of how she managed to get out of the car. Enthralled by her story, I sat forward in my chair and took a gulp of wine as she told me that what happened next was like something out of a nightmare.

'I'll never forget the feeling of shock as I looked back at this battered Jeep. There I was, still trapped in the driver's seat, unconscious and bleeding. I just stood there, staring, scared and confused. I wanted to pinch myself to wake up. How could I be in two places at the same time?'

Carol had no idea how long she stood there, but the next thing she knew there were people all around her. At first she thought they must be the ambulance crew and emergency services, but no one seemed to be showing any signs of urgency.

'I became really frustrated by them,' she said. 'I was shouting that there had been an accident, but they just smiled at me. And then I noticed a man among them who seemed very familiar.'

As the man came close, Carol recognised her grandfather, who had died when she was still a child. She gazed at him in shock and all she could remember of what he told her was that she should wait there with the Jeep and that he would wait with her. He held out his arms to her and she nestled into him, and felt the physical sensation of being cuddled by him. And then suddenly people were trying to get to her, but to the other Carol, the one who was still in the Jeep. She watched as the ambulance men laid her on the ground, pressing down on her chest in rapid movements. Then her grandfather turned to her and said, 'It's not your time to go, Carol. Go back. Tell your mum and dad I'm fine and that I love them. We will be together again, but not now.'

Seeing that Carol was very moved by recalling this encounter, I reached forward and squeezed her hand to reassure her.

'You do believe me, don't you?' she asked.

And of course I did.

When we hear of such experiences, from very ordinary people with little or no religious conviction, it seems impossible to deny the existence of the afterlife. Despite having no belief in the spirit world beforehand, these people encountered evidence of it during the time their souls left their bodies. No doubt they returned to Earth rather different, knowing as they now did that life is not just about the physical experience, but also a life yet to come.

At nine o'clock in the morning on a dull, drizzly December day I answered the phone with a sense of dread that sadly proved to be well founded. I struggled to hear my mum's hushed tones as she tried to choke back tears before telling me, 'I've had a call from the hospital. Grace died an hour ago.'

Half an hour later, I found myself in a side room off a ward in Southend Hospital, gazing at the form of my dear great-auntie, who looked as though she'd simply fallen asleep in front of me. She'd had cancer and had spent the last couple of weeks of her life in hospital. I'd been there every day with her, willing her to get better and asking the spirit people – my nan, granddad and uncle Roy – to gather close from the spirit world and make her well. But I guess I knew her passing was inevitable. No doubt many would say that, at the age of 76, she had had a good life or a 'good innings', but I'm sure that all those who have lost elderly relatives would agree that the fact that they made it into old age comes as little comfort – we still mourn and grieve as intensely as with the loss of any other beloved person.

Shortly before she died, Grace told me that she had seen her sister – my nan – and her father at her bedside, which gave me great comfort at the time. And now her journey had come to an end, although I felt incredibly sad and lost, I was relieved that she was free from pain and suffering. I sat there with her for some time, stroking her hair, looking at her face, holding her hand, knowing this would be the last time I would see her physically – and yet hoping that before long I would receive a spirit contact from her. But I knew I would miss her physical touch, the sound of her voice, the smell of her perfume and even the smell of Polo mints and perming lotion that I associated with her so strongly – all those little things that made her, well, just her.

After sitting with her like this for some time, I sensed that this was no longer my Auntie Grace. The humour, the zest for life, the ability to make me laugh and cry all within one sentence, the very force which made her who she was, had withdrawn and moved on. Her personality, her memories and her philosophy on life had also moved far away from the body I was mourning over. I remember standing up, kissing her lightly on the forehead and whispering into her ear, 'Bye

bye for now,' entirely convinced that we would meet again one day, when the time was right.

As I walked from the hospital back to my car, the sun began to shine and I was filled with a mix of emotions – a profound sadness that pressed heavily against my chest as though trying to stop me from breathing, and also, strangely, a sense of happiness. I knew that although we would grieve and feel bereft as we planned her funeral, for Auntie Grace on the other side it would be like a birthday party. I gained great comfort from this as I drove home, thinking of the conversations she would already be having with my nan – her sister – as they caught up on years of separation, and I couldn't help smiling as I imagined them all doing the hokey-cokey as I'd seen them do so many times as a child.

As many of you will appreciate, it can sometimes seem that getting older is both a blessing and a curse – we might gain maturity, wisdom and financial stability, but the older we become the more family members, friends and partners we lose. But death is as much a part of life as living itself and can't be ignored or avoided. Embracing this reality can be incredibly empowering as we recognise that death is not something to fear but to accept. It is the beginning of a new life and myriad new experiences in our true home, the spirit world. Peter Pan was right, death is an awfully big adventure!

This was never more apparent to me than when I was working a number of years ago at London's College of Psychic Studies, based in a beautiful part of South Kensington. I've always enjoyed my involvement at the college. Beyond the elegant white pillars framing the polished, jet-black entrance door lies a diverse and progressive environment, which is matched equally by the varied and interesting people that attend it. My work there at the time included holding psychic development courses and giving demonstrations, lectures and one-to-one consultations.

I clearly remember my first encounter with Malcolm. It was a bitterly cold winter's day and I was ensconced in my cosy room at the college having recently completed a reading for a young Portuguese woman. Glancing down at my watch I realised that my last appointment would be waiting for me. When I looked into the corridor, I saw an elderly man, sitting hunched over with his head in his hands, and I couldn't help thinking that he resembled a large pile of laundry, so plentiful were the layers of clothing that swamped his body. I introduced myself and we went back into my room. After some persuasion, Malcolm parted with his coat, although I convinced him to do so only by repeating my grandmother's advice that if he didn't then he wouldn't feel the benefit when he went back outside.

We sat down and I began the reading. In a shot, I heard myself saying, 'I have a woman here, I have the name of Rose.' He looked at me, more in disbelief than shock, his eyes moist with tears and I immediately knew that Rose was of course his dear departed wife. It always amazes me when some readings feel completely effortless, as though all I need to do is speak and the spirit people take control. Now, names, dates, facts and poignant memories flowed through me, each statement I made being greeted with more and more enthusiasm by Malcolm. It continued this way for a good forty-five minutes, and then towards the end of the reading I became very much aware that Malcolm had with him, some-where about his person, a lock of his Rose's hair. I asked him whether the hair was tied with pink ribbon, he then reached into his trouser pocket and handed me a lock of snow-white hair encircled by the same pink ribbon I had envisaged. I held the lock in my hands, hoping that holding something so tangible would invoke an even stronger connection.

As I closed my eyes to receive more information, I felt something quite shocking and found myself becoming increasingly emotional. I was very reluctant to share my thoughts with Malcolm, but then I heard his wife say something clearly in my left ear, before adding, 'Tell him. It's all right, you can tell him.'

When faced with difficult information, I obviously have to be incredibly careful not to cause pain or distress to my sitter. I was told many years ago by my tutor that everything I offer to a client should always enable and not disable them, and yet so insistent was Rose's voice that I knew I somehow had to find a way of expressing her sentiments without upsetting Malcolm. But I couldn't find the words, so I skirted around the subject, asking Malcolm various questions such as whether he had felt under the weather recently. After a little while he looked me squarely in the eye and said, 'It's OK, son, you can say it. I know I'm dying.' I then told him exactly what Rose had said to me, that he would be joining her soon and she would be waiting for him.

It transpired that, while nursing Rose, Malcolm had also been diagnosed with terminal cancer. But he'd kept this news from her, choosing instead to devote all his time and efforts to her care and comfort. He explained to me afterwards that he hadn't requested any treatment for his own illness while Rose was alive as he wanted to shield her from any additional pain. He promised himself that he would have treatment after she had gone. But he felt so desolate and lost when she died that he continued to deny himself medical care and had now been given just six weeks to live.

At this point Malcolm confided in me that all he'd needed to know from this reading was what I had conveyed to him, that his wife would be waiting for him. As I showed him out and led him downstairs to the foyer, he thanked me for the work I'd done and then asked if he could give me a hug. As we held each other, I felt his body begin to shake and I let him cry for a while as I held him. He then told me, 'I'll try to get back and tell you that I've met her, and if I can, I'll tell you something about heaven too.'

I waved goodbye to Malcolm and collected my coat in readiness to go home. I have to confess that I thought little more about this particular connection in the days and weeks afterwards because, although this might sound a bit heartless or detached, I am so busy that it just isn't possible to spend time reflecting on every reading. Rather like a doctor, the focus always has to be on the present patient – or in my case, client – so I put the story of Malcolm to one side, unsuspecting of the experience that lay ahead.

People who know of my work have generally seen me on television or at public demonstrations, but I also work in a far more diverse way, and out of the public eye. An example of this is the practice of automatic writing, a fascinating skill I learned over twenty years ago. The process itself is incredibly simple, placing the point of a pen lightly onto a sheet of white paper and allowing the spirit people to manipulate it to create their own messages to their intended recipient – as though they were letters from heaven.

A year or so after that meeting with Malcolm, while sitting quietly in my workroom, I suddenly felt inspired to pick up a pen and allow the spirit world to write through me. I'm quite used to working in this way, often receiving poetry, verse or philosophical ideas that I use later in addresses and talks. But this time something rather peculiar happened. The pen started to move and as I glanced down I saw the words, 'Malcolm and Rose here.' Not instantly recalling the previous experience, I sent up a thought, 'Malcolm and Rose who?' Like a flash the answer came into my mind, 'Malcolm and

Rose from the college in London.' I then of course remembered the plight of the old man and the loss of his beloved wife. Although it might seem hard to believe, there followed a lengthy message from Malcolm, given via the process of automatic writing, and I set out below the words he gave me.

'I died and she was there. I closed my eyes, felt myself lifting, lifting far and away from that old body. There was light all around me. I felt so young and then my eyes saw her, my lovely Rose. She was young again too and now we are together. I said I'd come back and let you know what it's like here and if it was true – and it is, every bit of it. I've met my mum and my dad and even my baby brother – we're all here. There are people I don't know, but they all seem to know me. When I first got here, they shook my hand, called me by name and made me feel very welcome.

'Things are quicker here; nothing takes long at all. If you want to be somewhere, you can be there in a flash. We're often by the river you know, me and my Rose, with the ducks, just like we did when we were younger. Nothing hurts any more, things are much clearer. Me and Rose back together again.'

The writing stopped abruptly and I found my hand twisting, as though it were being held firmly by an unseen hand, which then began to draw. It drew a hill and a sun, a stream and a small house, surrounded by flowers – lots and lots of flowers – and then words came again:

'That's where we live, me and Rose.'

As I read each of these words as it appeared on the paper, I found myself becoming excited and emotional. A thousand thoughts whirred round in my mind, not least that I had achieved an extraordinary direct link to the spirit world. I wanted to know how it was to pass over, what spirit life was really like, as well as wanting to gain a fuller understanding of Malcolm's experience. Then, as though he'd read my mind, one more paragraph began to flow, like a parting gift from him to me.

'When I died, I saw angels. Beautiful and bright. They smiled at me and made me feel so at home. I've only seen them a few times since, but they're there if we ask them to come, and when we can't see them we can feel them, just like you can too.

'Life can be hard, dying is easy. Thanks for everything, Malcolm and Rose.'

Much has been written about grief, how we feel about the tremendous loss and pain caused by imposed separation. The method of a loved one's passing is also of great importance. It can be comforting to think that someone died quickly and peacefully in their sleep, or extremely distressing that another had to endure a lengthy and painful passing. But I wonder how many people take the time to question how it might actually be to die. What exactly is this process? We know how it is to be born and how the physical body is conceived, but even those of us convinced of an afterlife rarely truly consider the process of death.

I am certainly someone who thinks about how it might be. It struck me one day that if I can receive evidential communication from the loved ones of my clients and those who attend demonstrations, I must also be able to receive the answers to my questions from those who guide me and love me. So I decided to ask them.

This notion came to me during a time when I was visiting the valleys of South Wales. Every January I go there to give four or five demonstrations, from Brecon to Cwmbran, organised by a lovely woman called Jenny, who helps run a spiritual group.

I knew that if I was to ask those who guide me about the process of death, the answers I received would be both special and profound, and I therefore wanted to be in just the right surroundings. So I got up at 6.30 the next morning and left the B&B where I was staying, closing the front door quietly so as not to disturb the other guests.

Being a man from a suburban area, I ensured before I left for Wales that I would be suitably attired for the countryside, investing time and money in buying the necessary gear. This grey, drizzly morning provided the perfect opportunity to try it all out. Duly clad in my smart new waxed jacket and water-proof trousers over pristine wellington boots, I then spent a little too much time making sure my new flat cap was placed at just the right angle on my head. I expect I still looked like a proper townie, but undeterred I set off in my car to Sugarloaf Mountain, situated to the north-west of Abergavenny.

By the time I got there, the sun was struggling to appear through the clouds, but even when it did show itself it was altogether too half-hearted in the effort. I took myself for a walk, drinking in the beautiful landscape. There's some-thing very special about South Wales, not only for its beauty, but also its extraordinary serenity. At that time of the year, some might describe the landscape as a little bleak, but I saw something else as I surveyed the territory all around me: life. Everywhere there was life, which continued to blossom and evolve despite the harsh winds and bitter temperature. No other people were around and I was completely at one with my surroundings. And then, as though reaching out directly to the whole universe, I silently asked the question: 'What is it like to die? Friends in the other world, share with me your knowledge.'

In an instant, as I'm sure the spirit world was aware of my plans, I immediately felt words and impressions begin to tumble into my mind. My legs suddenly became incredibly weak, so I sat down cross-legged on the wet earth. I kept my eyes open throughout this experience, gazing at the greyness of the sky and the damp greenness all around me; it was the most beautiful view I had ever seen. I felt myself entering into an altered state of consciousness, as if I were weightless and wrapped in cotton wool. And then the messages I was receiving began to gain clarity.

Allow me to express to you, from the impressions I received that day, how it might feel to return home to the spirit world after physical death. From the moment our bodies cease to function, pain is non-existent. The faculties of our minds are restored. All lust, greed and malice ebb away from us, as determined as the coastal tides. We are welcomed back to the power of all creativity, whole and complete, all disabilities, abnormalities and illnesses having been healed instantaneously.

Then the journey begins, through time and space, moving faster than the speed of light. Visions and experiences during this journey are unique to each person, but always positive, directed by and an expression of our individual souls. On reaching the spiritual realm, we are drawn to areas where we will feel most comfortable, according to our life experiences. The tribesman will enter his idea of heaven, the mountain man another, the western man somewhere that is more in keeping with his structured physical world; yet all of these places abound with beauty, light, colour and nature. All life is there: animals, flora and fauna of every imaginable description. But beyond all that you might see, is continuous and eternal love – the love that emanates from us and the love we receive from all who share this place with us. We are reunited with those we have loved; babies and children are cared for and nurtured by their family members on the other side; no one is ever lost in pain or in darkness. To die is to be reunited, made whole, and it heralds a brand new beginning, a new life – a spirit life.

I cannot begin to express how powerfully this revelation came to me, but I can tell you that it made me feel amazing. At that moment, honestly and completely, all fear of death left me, now and forever.

After a while I returned to everyday consciousness, and found myself very cold and wet as it must have been raining heavily during this time of revelation. My cloth cap afforded me little protection and I was soaked through to the skin. But I didn't care. My experience on Sugarloaf Mountain will remain with me always.

I don't consider myself to be a selfish person, but sometimes I wonder about it because I find myself seeking out ever more spiritual journeys like these – it just feels so wonderful, almost like getting a small lottery win on a regular basis! I feel myself incredibly lucky to have such fabulous and life-changing experiences.

It was not long after my visit to Sugarloaf Mountain that I attended what had been billed as 'a masterclass for mediumship development'. I have to confess I was rather nervous about this as I hadn't been on a course as a student for many years. The masterclass was held at my own development studio and the tutor and medium was a woman I've known for a long time, Mavis Pittilla. She is highly regarded in this field, having helped train many excellent workers in philosophy, mediumship and teaching.

During the course, Mavis spoke of the influences the spirit world can have on our lives, and a key section of her lecture really resonated with me. She said, 'You do know, don't you, that it's possible to make an appointment with the spirit world? For instance, if you ever find yourself entering an historic building, don't be afraid to send up a thought to the spirit people and ask that one of them might meet you to give you a guided tour of the premises.'

I couldn't help smiling to myself, totally fascinated by the whole idea. As many of you know, I seem to live my life out of a suitcase, travelling from town to town, country to country, and it wasn't long before I found myself standing outside Lincoln's magnificent gothic cathedral. I stayed for a while in the grounds, taking in this glorious vision and then, glancing at my watch, I realised I had at least four hours before I needed to get ready for the evening's demonstration in Lincoln's theatre. As I stood there I was reminded of Mavis's advice, so I sent up a thought asking if anybody in the other world who had knowledge of the cathedral would show me what it was like many years ago. This way I might glean far more information than I'd find in any tourist book – and free of charge at that! I added to my request that perhaps they would kindly meet me at the entrance.

As I passed through the majestic 11th-century Norman doors, it was clear that nobody was there to greet me. Unperturbed, I walked on into this hallowed place and stood for some time gazing up at the fabulous architecture, trying to take in as much as possible. The ceiling seemed to go on forever, as though reaching to touch the heavens. It was there, while gazing up, that I heard a voice behind me, 'Welcome.' I spun round, expecting to find one of the church wardens, but no one was there. Then the voice came again, 'Welcome, my son.'

Doing the work I do, you might expect me to hear voices coming out of mid-air on a daily basis. But I have to confess this one took me by surprise. I realised that Mavis had been right and my request for assistance and a guided tour had indeed been granted.

For the moment, however, the voice spoke no more, so I continued to wander around this incredible building, taking in every sight and smell and soaking up its ancient atmosphere. I must have looked a little pleased with myself as I smiled aimlessly throughout, but I didn't care who saw – I was having another one of my adventures!

As I walked up one of the aisles and turned right, I stood in awe before the most magnificent stained glass window. The exquisite craftsmanship was impressive enough, but it's difficult to describe the vibrant colours of the glass and how they were reflected onto the flagstone floor by the sun shining in brightly from outside. I purposely stood on the coloured reflections and closed my eyes. I can only describe the feeling I experienced as one of pure healing. It was as though each coloured ray was having a profound effect on me, physically, mentally and spiritually. I wanted to raise my arms in the air, spin round on the spot and cry out in joy. Luckily, I managed to rein in this impulse.

And then I heard the voice again, 'Beautiful, isn't it?' But this time the words were accompanied by a vision, and there before me was a young monk. From his unlined face and clear green eyes, he appeared to be in his mid-twenties. He had dark red hair, bare feet and was wearing a simple hessian robe. I'm not sure what order he was from, though I later learned that Bishop Remegius, who built the cathedral in 1092, was a Benedictine monk. I sensed that the man before me had lived during the 14th century and I somehow knew that we had met before. An overwhelming sense of love emanated from him towards me and I sent a simple thought to him, 'Thank you, friend, for coming. Thank you for allowing me to see you. I'm so pleased you have joined me. What can you show me, what can you tell me about this place?'

With that, as though I was being led by an unseen force, the journey began. He took me through every nook and cranny of this beautiful place, offering historical facts and insights into each window, carving, statue and resting place – far more information than I would have learned from any guidebook. But there was another big difference; it was not only dry facts he imparted, but also emotions, the happiness, sadness, triumph and tragedy pertaining to each point of interest. I found myself becoming increasingly tactile, wanting to touch every surface of the building, revelling in the sense of instant knowingness that came from everything I laid my hands on. Luckily, there weren't many people about, otherwise my urge to touch everything I saw might have caused a few problems!

My friend led me into the cloister, where I sensed many pious men walking in silent meditation. I felt their complete devotion so powerfully that it brought a tear to my eye.

After a while, I became a little weary and didn't think my friend would mind if I took a break. I felt him drift away as I re-entered my normal state of consciousness and made my way to the cathedral's canteen, where I ordered a cup of tea and a large slice of chocolate cake – one of my greatest indulgences. I saw on my mobile phone that I had four missed calls, but tempted as I was to listen to my messages, I thought it would be far more interesting to continue to receive messages from the other world, and so promised myself another hour of exploration.

I went back into the main body of the cathedral and sat down on one of the long, cold, wooden pews. I made myself comfortable and closed my eyes, sending a thought to the other world asking my new friend to return. Instantaneously, I felt his presence once again, not next to me but sitting in one of the pews on the other side of the aisle. His head was bowed as if in silent prayer and I watched him for a while. He finally turned towards me, and as he did I saw that his face had changed – he was older now and his hair had turned white, his green eyes clouded by the passage of time. He looked weak and forlorn and seeing him this way shocked me a little, but I realised that this was part of what he wanted to convey to me, so I surrendered myself to the experience. I saw him rise from his seat and walk to the nave, where he stood looking back at me. It was then that his voice came to me again, loud and clear, 'Let me share with you who I am and why I am here.'

As his words resonated within me, I suddenly knew that to gain the most from what was to come, I would have to look through my friend's eyes and that he and I would need to become as one – a merging of souls, our thoughts and our hearts entwined. Only then would I fully experience what he himself had experienced.

I made a conscious decision that I wanted to go ahead, to allow my soul to merge with his. Then, at will, I let my consciousness expand so that my mind was able to blend with his. Although my physical body remained exactly where it was, I felt my spirit lift from the pew and in less than a second I knew that I was part of him, now looking out through his eyes. His hair was on my head, his rough, hessian robe hung on my body.

The next sensation I became aware of was that of complete fear. I was also incredibly cold and began to shake. Then I heard voices all around, calling me, but not by my own name. They called me Thomas, the name of my spirit visitor, and they were from the same era as him. 'Thomas,' they urged, 'it's time to leave.'

In an instant, Thomas's story became clear to me. Because our minds had entwined, there was no need for anything to

be explained – I knew his story and his plight. He entered
the monastery at a very young age, after his parents died in a
house fire. He himself had been badly scarred by the flames,
but had survived this dreadful ordeal. The monastery then
became his entire life. For over forty years, he selflessly gave
every part of his being in the service of God and to his love
of the Church, bringing religious instruction, care and suste-
nance to all those who came asking for help.

Eventually, change came to the cathedral. New ideas and
practices were introduced and monks who were more progressive were invited to join the order. With each new arrival, one
of Thomas's old brethren was asked to leave or to relocate
to churches in the surrounding area, until there came a point
when only Thomas remained from the 'old school'. Then,
inevitably, one day he too was asked to continue his service
to the Church elsewhere.

I was now intensely aware of Thomas's all-consuming
grief, fear and disbelief at having to leave the only home he
had ever known. Standing in the centre of the cathedral, he
and I combined as one, Thomas tilted his head, gazing up
into the colours of the stained glass windows and beyond to
the majestic high ceilings, taking in every last glimpse of this
most beautiful house of God. His pain and loss were insurmountable and I felt him weep. I was completely powerless,
and then I felt his legs give out from under him, a pain crash-
ing through his chest as he fell to the cathedral floor. . . and
I felt the life force leave his body. I have often heard how
it's possible to die from a broken heart and this, I believe, is
exactly how Thomas passed away.

I could feel his face against the cold floor as he lay there.
Then there was a shift within his body and I felt his spirit rise,
leaping easily and joyfully from his body. It moved onwards
and upwards, seeing the cathedral from a perspective he had

never experienced in all his years in this place. There was a pause as he was once more drawn to the mesmerising deep reds, mauves and sunlight yellows of a stained glass window. Then Thomas's spirit seemed to fly into the coloured rays and out through the window itself, where it was consumed by a dazzling white light.

It was at this point that I became aware of my own physical self, still sitting on the same pew. Despite the fact that I was now back in my own body, I was completely aware that I had experienced something of Thomas's life – and more extraordinarily his death – as well as the sheer exhilaration that he felt to be free from his body. When I saw his spirit leave the cathedral, his body was young and vibrant again, his hair again a striking red, and although I didn't see them, I knew that his gentle, kind eyes were as clear and as green as when he had first shown himself to me.

Just as I was preparing to leave the cathedral, having checked my mobile for yet more missed calls, I heard the voice of Thomas again. 'For me,' he said, 'this place is like heaven. I am now its caretaker and I bring the light of heaven here within these walls, so that those who seek can find truth.'

As I left, I knew that Lincoln Cathedral was in safe hands. Thomas had indeed passed and entered the realms of the spirit world, but it had then been his decision to spend much of his time near the physical world, to make a difference in the place he still called home. When I took Mavis's advice and asked that someone from the other world might meet and guide me, it was only fitting that Thomas should do the honours.

3
Onwards and Upwards

'I've seen and met angels wearing the disguise of ordinary people living ordinary lives.'

Tracy Chapman – singer-songwriter

Some years ago, while watching the movie about Tina Turner's rise to fame, *What's Love Got to Do with It*, I was touched by the performance of Rae'Ven Larrymore Kelly, the young actress who played Tina Turner as a child. In a scene where she and the rest of the church choir were performing the song 'This Little Light of Mine', Rae'Ven stood out a mile as she belted out the lyrics, smiling and swaying the whole way through, putting every part of her being into the performance. 'This little light of mine, I'm gonna let it shine, let it shine, let it shine, let it shine.' These simple words resounded deep within me, for they reaffirmed my already strongly-held belief that each of us is here in this world to let our light shine and share it with others.

More recently, I discovered in Marianne Williamson's book *A Return to Love: Reflections on the Principles of 'A Course in Miracles'* the following much-quoted passage, which elaborates on the same message – and puts it more eloquently than ever I could!

Our deepest fear is not that we are inadequate.
Our deepest fear is that we are powerful beyond measure.
It is our light, not our darkness, that most frightens us.

We ask ourselves: who am I to be brilliant, gorgeous,
talented and fabulous?
Actually, who are you not to be?
You are a child of God.
Your playing small does not serve the world.
There is nothing enlightened about shrinking,
so that other people won't feel insecure around you.
We were born to make manifest the glory of God that
is within us.
It is not just in some of us; it is in everyone.
And as we let our own light shine, we unconsciously
give other people permission to do the same.
As we are liberated from our fear, our presence
automatically liberates others.

These powerful words beautifully illustrate a part of my
philosophy, which is that the reason we are here walking on
the Earth is to enrich our soul and serve our brothers and
sisters who share the planet with us. Each life lived here is
but a small journey towards enhancing the vast tapestry that
is the sum total of all our lives.

During my psychic development my tutor would often
remind me, 'Tony, you are a spirit being having a physical
experience and not a physical being having a spiritual experience.' From this viewpoint, it is obviously far easier to get
to grips with the concepts of life after death and each of us
having limitless spiritual potential. As my journey of development continued, I would often be confronted by other
people's opinions and concepts of spirituality, and on more
than one occasion it was suggested to me that each of us
chooses the life we wish to live while here on the Earth. I can
go along with this to an extent. For example, I believe that
I chose to be born to my mum and dad and to be brother to

my sister Lorraine. I can also accept that it was necessary for me to be born in east London, brought up in Essex and from the age of sixteen attend the local spiritualist church, so that I might receive the guidance and training to get me to the point where I am now – to write this book and share with you my experiences so far.

I began to struggle, however, when it was occasionally suggested to me that people who have experienced terribly difficult lives have chosen these lives for themselves. The more I thought about this, the more I started to wonder and question. Why would people who were experiencing extreme hardship – babies born in war-torn or poverty-stricken countries, children battling cancer and other diseases, the elderly and infirm suffering years of dementia with no real quality of life – why would any one of these spirits have specifically chosen to go through such ordeals? Surely such severe mental and physical deprivation could not be 'necessary' for the further development of the soul? An experience I had a few years ago, when giving a private reading, might help to shed light on the question.

Lesley was a tall, blonde, elegantly-dressed woman in her late thirties, who journeyed down from Scotland to see me, having been on my waiting list for a private appointment for a couple of years. Despite her attractive appearance and a lovely, subtle waft of perfume as she walked into my studio, it felt as though a black cloud had followed her into the room. As I greeted her, I recognised the intense pain and loss in her eyes and knew at once that she had lost a child. We exchanged a few brief pleasantries about her trip, but I was well aware that she hadn't come all this way to make small talk, and so we made ourselves comfortable, ready to begin.

I closed my eyes and proceeded to link into the spirit world, within moments finding myself describing a nine-year-old girl with short red hair, a pale complexion and the name of Sarah. Before I had a chance to ask Lesley if she recognised such a girl, I heard her softly begin to cry. I understood the young girl to be her daughter and so moved on with the reading. Information flowed through, memories involving holidays in Florida, a baby brother who had been born after Sarah had passed and many other positive affirmations of the young spirit girl's return to her mother. Towards the end of the session, I found myself saying, 'Your daughter is very anxious for you to know that she never wanted to leave you. It is important that you understand that the way she passed was not of her choosing and that if she could be here with you now she would be.' After these words were spoken, Lesley dissolved into tears.

As we sat over a cup of tea at the end of the session, Lesley explained that her daughter Sarah had died of a brain tumour three years before, and since that time Lesley had struggled in vain to come to terms with this terrible loss. She went on to tell me that her daughter had also come through during a Spiritualist Church service shortly after her passing. The medium had accurately described Sarah and said she was well in the other world, but then went on to state that she had chosen to die at that time and in the way she did as part of her spiritual development. Not only this, but she had also gone so as to help Lesley to learn and grow from the experience.

As I silently gave her more tissues, Lesley told me, 'When I left the church I felt so confused. I was elated that Sarah had come through, but no closer at all to understanding why she had had to die in that way. Did she not love me enough to stay here with me?' Although she didn't say so directly, I knew that Lesley had also been tormenting herself about what awful things she must have done to deserve to be 'taught a lesson' in such a terrible way.

I sat for a moment before I answered, mulling over the philosophies of some of my tutors and peers that all life is a life lesson, that we choose when we will live and when we will die and also our method of despatch. But now, hearing Lesley's story and with Sarah's words still resonating within me – 'I didn't want to leave you, I didn't mean to go that way' – I couldn't help question this way of thinking. I found myself repeating Sarah's words to Lesley and emphasising that her daughter had seemed very anxious to set the record straight, for which Lesley appeared both relieved and grateful.

While I'm glad that the reading was comforting to Lesley, I must admit that it did much for me too, in that it caused me to amend my way of thinking. I now realise that brain tumours and the like just happen; there's no puppet master in the sky making some of us ill and reprieving the rest. It is now crystal clear to me that no small child would want to leave their parents and all the wonderful experiences that life has to offer at such a young and precious age. I believe that each of us, without exception, chooses to come into this world hoping for a good, healthy and long life, to gain the most we can from the journey and to spread as much joy as we can while we are here. But we are nonetheless born into a physical body and all the limitations that go with it – things can and do go wrong with it, in just the same way as random accidents happen. Not everything is preordained.

Aware of how the experience with Lesley had changed my opinion, I began to reconsider many other ideas, asking myself major questions such as, if God exists why does He allow terrible things to happen, like war, famine and disease? No doubt many of us have at times wondered whether bad things happen in order to teach us a lesson or to show God's dissatisfaction; or whether it might be possible that, on some deeper karmic level, we created certain difficult situations ourselves, as a part of our life experience, so that we might overcome that which might seem insurmountable.

Wars happen because man sometimes has an inability to resolve differences peaceably, acting out of revenge and anger rather than forgiveness and love. God does not create war and neither would He take sides; He would simply want balance to be restored, so that we might continue with our evolution.

The way I view life and spirituality shifts and broadens continuously as I continue to develop my insight and psychic awareness. As I write this book, my philosophy is that each of us comes from the spiritual world, having elected to be born here in the physical world. None of us is in any way forced, it is our choice and it is no accident that we find ourselves in the place where we are today. For us to have an earth life experience, we need a vehicle in which our soul might travel the physical world, and this, of course, is the human body. But if a car on occasion breaks down, it's hardly surprising that an entity as infinitely complex as the human body will sometimes similarly malfunction. So if someone passes tragically young, it was not by choice or some sort of 'payback'. They would have wanted to live here in this world for many, many years, before ultimately taking back with them to the spirit world myriad tales of all the wondrous experiences that Earth has to offer.

One of the most powerful revelations I have ever received came during a meditation as I sat at home listening to the music of Krishna Das, an extraordinary man who expresses through song his devotion to the philosophies relating to Krishna. If you listen to his work, I feel sure you'll be touched in the same way I have been.

On this particular day, as I was lost in the music and my meditation, words suddenly tumbled into my mind, as though someone were addressing me specifically: 'Each of you is an eternal being. You have always existed and will always exist. Each of you is a part of the Great Spirit. All knowledge lies within you, within the deepest part of you. The purpose of life is to bring forth this knowledge into the conscious mind. Once knowledge has been remembered, formulated and spoken in words, observe the effects of its truth – just as the ripples of a stone thrown into the water, spiritual truth reaches out and impacts positively on all who are ready to embrace it.'

These words came to me with such clarity that they almost took my breath away. My heart was beating fast and I felt a tremendous sense of elation. I was afraid to open my eyes in case I broke this powerful link with the other world, and so I stayed as I was for some minutes, hoping and praying that more revelations would be received. The warm, guttural sounds of the music vibrated through my entire being and I couldn't remember a time when I felt more blessed.

Inevitably, the experience came to an end and I found myself back in the room. The first thing I did was take a notepad and write down the words that had come through to me so clearly.

There have been many times in my life when I have not just been blessed with messages from the spirit world for others, but have also been fortunate enough to feel the presence of those who guide and guard me, as well as more advanced spirit beings wishing to bring light and understanding to our world. Many times I have been moved to tears, for the words and visions I receive are always accompanied by the sense of unconditional love and the reaffirmation that we are all members of a band of spirit beings whose common interest is in bringing truths and blessings back to the physical world. Every one of us has the capability to achieve this.

Going back to Lesley and her daughter who passed away, sadly their story is not unique. I am confronted by the issue of serious physical illness or injury almost every day, whether in the course of giving public demonstrations or personal one-to-one readings. I probably find myself referring to the method of someone's passing at least ten times a day, because I believe this information is an important part of their survival evidence. Typically, when I'm giving a public demonstration of mediumship, I rarely go directly to the recipient of a message, preferring instead to focus all my energies at that moment on the spirit person who is trying to come through. I invariably feel a spirit presence on my left-hand side, and as soon as I recognise they are there and are prepared for me to describe them, I surrender my mind to them and allow their thoughts and feelings to tumble into my conscious mind. Because I've been working in this way for so many years, I've become used to expecting certain pieces of information to come through. If anyone has seen me in a demonstration, they will know that a typical description might start like this: 'I have a young man here. I know he has not long passed. He feels around thirty-six. I know he passed from a brain tumour. He gives me the name Martin.' Then at this point I would ask, 'Who here in the audience understands this?' Invariably, someone will put their hand up or call out to get my attention. I then speak to that person, and once I'm happy that the information is indeed for them – which I am readily able to tell as the spirit next to me gets excited too – I'm able to pass on messages, shared memories and evidential statements, all of which I hope add up to a clear indication to the recipient, and also the audience, that communication is being received from the other world.

As you might appreciate, the fact that this young man had passed from a brain tumour is a vital piece of information when trying to identify him to his loved one in the audience. I've been asked a thousand times how I receive this information and I'm happy to share with you that this happens in two main ways. The first is an overwhelming feeling that comes over me, as though someone from the other world is sharing my mind. In the case of Martin above, I would know there was an issue with his brain before he passed, and then all my attention would shift to my own brain. I might sense a dull, aching feeling in a certain area of my brain, in which case I would know that there was a tumour. If, however, the sensation was accompanied by a sharp, spiky feeling, I would interpret that as a brain haemorrhage.

Secondly, I will also see information – for example, the name of Martin would be written in my mind's eye, as if on an imaginary notepad. Sometimes I will also see writing on a chalk board, and if this happens I will know that the name links back many years. If I see a name written in a child's hand, I know this, of course, will be the name of a child. If I see the name written in a typed font, I will know this name links to a police investigation, and so on. But just as there are a thousand more references that are unique to me, any of you can work towards receiving spirit information in a way that is unique to you.

Once, I was giving a week-long development course for twenty or so students at the a college in Essex, a beautiful gothic manor house set in its own grounds, owned and run by the Spiritualist National Union for the purpose of providing people with spiritual understanding and psychic and medium-ship development. Towards the end of the week, I decided to use one of the sessions for philosophical debate and general discussion. All manner of topics were raised, and in a lively exchange we spoke of everything from the merits of spiritual healing and reiki to the origins of the human soul.

At one point, a young woman named Kate asked if she could speak. Although she had participated well in the class all week and seemed positive and energetic, I'd noticed her somewhat drawn face and ultra-slim body, which looked swamped by the clothes she was wearing. Kate explained how she felt she'd been guided to take this particular course and how much she'd learned from it and enjoyed it. Then she became choked with emotion as she confided to the group that she had almost not made the course because she'd been receiving treatment for cancer. Only days before, she'd been given positive indications from her consultant that the treatment had been successful, so at the last moment she packed her bags, feeling better than she had in many months, and travelled to join us.

All of this I found most inspiring, and as I surveyed the group I saw many of them had been similarly touched by her journey. But at this point she went on to say how she wanted publicly to thank the spirit world for giving her her cancer. A little shocked, I asked her to explain what she meant. She told us, 'I believe they made me ill to get me to evaluate my life, to sit up and realise what living is all about. I somehow sensed that they wouldn't take me over to the other world, but it was definitely my wake-up call and I will be looking at life differently from now on.'

It took me a moment to formulate my own thoughts, and as much as I didn't want to offend her, or belittle her comments in front of the rest of the group, I felt I had to explain my belief that the spirit people would have had no part to play in her cancer. They certainly would never have chosen such a drastic course of action to inspire her to look inwardly and consider her life in a more spiritual way. Her illness was simply a malfunction of her physical body and nothing more than that. I was, however, incredibly pleased that she had turned a negative into a positive and I tried to instil in her that the spirit world would only want positive things for us – their desire would never be to create pain in our lives, but only to help, love and heal us.

Kate seemed to take this on board, but wanted to see me privately after the class. When the others had left, she asked me to explain my thoughts further. I re-emphasised my belief that the Great Spirit and inhabitants of the other world would never create illness within any of us as a means of punishment for some perceived sin on our part, or indeed as any kind of catalyst towards spiritual enlightenment. I could tell she was still struggling with this, as for some reason she had convinced herself that her illness had been created and given to her as some sort of karmic lesson. I suppose we all have a great need to find explanations for the unpleasant things that happen in our lives and I think this was just Kate's way of coping with something that was otherwise inexplicable.

I told her that to me it was inconceivable that those advanced beings who specifically come forward to help us would ever want to hurt us or bring us pain – and if this 'shock tactic' approach was their modus operandi they could surely never have attained an advanced level of enlightenment in the first place. Through all the spiritual communications I have received over the years, never once have I sensed pain or infirmity in the other world, which to me clearly indicates that illness dwells only in this world and has no part in the next. Our bodies are organic structures that can malfunction just like a motor car can – things go wrong either through wear and tear or, especially, if we don't take proper care and carry out regular maintenance.

Kate and I debated our opposing philosophies for so long that we missed lunch, and in the end had to agree to disagree. And you know, that was fine: I have never professed to have all the answers, but always try to speak straight from the heart. My truth is simple – it has to be, I'm no Einstein;

illness to me is something to be overcome, not embraced and I can see no need for physical suffering to be inflicted on us as though it were part of some kind of master plan as we travel this path through life.

Later that day, I gave a lecture at the college to about a hundred students. I had planned to talk of the history of spiritualism, but as I stood to address the participants with my lecture notes in my hand, I felt the pages fall from my fingers. Rather than rush to pick them up and put them back in order to commence my talk, I realised this was just the excuse I was looking for to abandon the planned lecture and set off in a different direction.

I simply stood there, with a hundred people staring at me and no doubt wondering why I was suddenly incapable of picking up a few pieces of paper. But I was no longer fully in this world. My body felt as light as a feather and I was compelled to close my eyes. I was aware of a being of light standing directly behind me, one of those who dwell in the angelic realm. At no point did I try to interfere with what was happening, instead submitting to and embracing the experience. Then, when I opened my mouth to speak, it was as if the words were being spoken through me, bypassing my conscious thoughts. Here is how I began:

'The Great Spirit is a beautiful, awe-inspiring, creative, gentle, parental, joyous, colourful and passionate universal power that links all life together, that gives unlimited potential to expand your consciousness. You may evolve in subtle ways over a long period of time as truths are gifted to you when you are ready to receive them. My friends, journey with me in your minds and try to appreciate that you are incredible and amazing, that you are beautiful spirit beings who have come to the physical world with good intention, wanting only to grow and to share while you are here.'

The lecture continued in this inspired fashion for a good hour. Much of its content now sits more in my heart than my memory, but one of the most moving sights I have ever witnessed was the look of complete joy and emotion on the faces of those present. It was obvious to me that this powerful effect had not only been created by the words spoken through me, but by how an extraordinary spirit being had been able to change the entire atmosphere of the room. It felt for a moment as though each of us had entered the kingdom of heaven.

Those of you who have been lucky enough to receive glimpses of this wondrous place will obviously be far more receptive to the true essence of the meaning carried by inspired words like those spoken during my lecture. But there are of course many people who are still unsure, or even cynical, about the existence of the afterlife. I fully understand that they might naturally ask, 'If the spirit world is such a wondrous, light and beautiful place, where we are all made whole and joy abounds, why on earth do we bother to spend time here?!'

I can only speak from my personal perspective, but I very much believe that we are all here to do our best. Even when life throws a spanner in the works, or it seems there is no light at the end of the tunnel, if we can learn to trust in the power that exists within us and believe that we are guided by unseen friends endeavouring to help us to triumph over adversity, then this will lead to the evolution of our souls. One of the greatest revelations we might receive is that we are a part of the universe and beings of limitless potential.

Often when I explain my thoughts on this to the new enquirer, their next question is, 'Why can't this evolution be achieved in the spirit world, rather than here on Earth?' To me the answer is quite clear: we can grow immensely through adversity. First, we must recognise that we are far more than flesh and blood while alive on Earth, and then we must learn to enable the true loving nature of our soul to triumph over greed, selfishness, jealousy, anger and intolerance. These negative traits might develop in our early upbringing or lie deep within the more primal aspects of human nature, but either way they are 'man-made', powerful and immensely difficult to overcome. Only the most highly developed of souls will be able to conquer such adversity, hence the need for the soul's progression via a lengthy and challenging journey that spans numerous Earth lives. No one ever said that the path to enlightenment would be an easy one!

Consider for a moment the great prophets and gurus of the past, many of whom chose to distance themselves from their communities, avoiding temptations of the flesh and spending vast amounts of time in solitude and meditation. Certainly for us here in the western world, this monastic kind of life would be difficult to follow, but I believe we should still strive to create moments of solitude when we can, for example, taking time out to appreciate nature, perhaps meditating briefly at our office desk or creating a quiet space in our homes where we can shut out all earthly distractions, even just for an hour or so. In these small ways, we will gradually attain a greater level of awareness, a greater appreciation that life is a blessing and that if we do our very best to share our laughter, our care and our kindness, we can triumph even in the face of adversity.

So in essence, once we have accepted that we are all a part of the Great Spirit, what better way is there to show our devotion to this loving force than by helping it to grow and evolve? By gaining greater spiritual understanding and being unafraid to bring light where there is darkness, love where there is hate and joy where there is sadness, we will attain enlightenment;

we will add to the brilliance of the whole and everyone will benefit from this expression of the soul's evolution.

I believe that those in the other world who watch over us, our guides and the angelic beings, assist us in our journey because they want us to attain the same level of enlightenment as themselves. They already know how difficult this path can be and are there with us to celebrate our triumphs and commiserate when we are burdened or full of angst. Just like a supportive older brother or sister, they take us under their wing, advise and look out for us. This is more than simply a belief: for me, based on my experiences, it is an absolute fact that spirits and angels do indeed walk with us throughout our lives.

Whether or not we consciously recognise this wonderful connection with our spirit helpers, each of us will be 'aware' of their assistance on a super-conscious level. When I say this, I mean that our own spirit within us fully understands that there are loving beings, brothers and sisters of the soul, who work alongside us. We may be more attuned to this during the time that we sleep, but then as we awaken we dip back into a state of mind that is limited by our brain. Depending on our life experiences, our conscious mind will either be open to expansion or firmly closed, and in the latter case might remain so for the duration of this current lifetime. So whether we can bring into our conscious thoughts an acknowledgement that there are angel beings who care for us will depend on our ability to reach an advanced level of enlightenment. It has often been said that these angels are God's messengers, and I am sure they are, but the messages they bring are designed to remind us of the truth that already lies deep within us.

I have been asked many times to make a distinction between spirit guides and angel beings. I appreciate that there is a commonly held belief among angel experts and enthusiasts that a specific number of archangels and lesser angels exist, each having separately defined roles to play within our lives, but to me it isn't so black and white. If we agree that our souls are constantly expanding and that the God force is also continuously evolving and becoming brighter, then any kind of limitation with regard to the number of angel beings just doesn't resonate with me. Surely the soul of each and every one of us can strive towards perfection.

Let us consider the path that might lead to a spirit being evolving into an angel. As I have said before, each of us is limitless in terms of potential and I therefore believe that we all have the capacity and opportunity to evolve spiritually to the advanced state of an angelic being. I recognise that this might go against many traditional angel teachings, but I can only talk of what is true to me. It is my great belief that we are free to become anything we wish and the only thing that separates us from those who dwell within the higher realms of the spirit world is the advancement of our spirit within. Each of us has the capacity to grow to such an extent that we too can become teachers, philosophers and enlightened beings.

The path that leads us to this involves many return visits to Earth, so that each time we are better prepared and able to express the knowledge and truths we have amassed. This may take us to a stage in our spiritual evolution where we recognise that no more can be learned or gained from living here on Earth and our time then may be spent solely within the spiritual realm. At this point in our journey, we might choose to become guardian spirits and through the wisdom acquired over many lifetimes help and inspire those who still need to experience a physical reality.

Through service to others, an even greater expansion of the spirit can occur, whereby the individual transcends all ego and need for praise and is elevated to the state of awareness that allows them to be nearer to the source of all creation – in my eyes, as an angelic being.

It has often been said that an angel has never incarnated here on Earth. I can't believe, however, that any one of us who has had a full array of earthly experiences and attained an advanced level of spiritual awareness would ever be unable to reach the status of an angelic being. So wherever in the world you might be as you read these words, regardless of your ethnic origin, background, financial status or sexual orientation, please recognise that you have the capability to transcend all negativity, all bias and all limitation. Through your experiences both here and in the other world, you have the potential to reach higher, to touch and merge with the advanced beings that continuously surround us.

4
Miracles, Wonders and Signs

'We are each of us angels with only one wing; and we can only fly by embracing one another.'

Luciano de Crescenzo

Because of the work I do, I sometimes feel I live my life between two worlds – this one and the next. But even though frequent encounters with spirits and angels are second nature to me, that doesn't mean I'm any less enthralled when I hear of other lives that have been touched by spirit.

I was once told the story of Crystal, an African woman in the Sudan whose husband had passed, leaving her to bring up four small children on her own. The village where she lived was regularly harassed by a band of local thugs and ex-military personnel, whose actions were more aggressive and intimidating each time they came in search of food, provisions and anything else they could lay their hands on. For a while, the attacks passed without violent incident, but when Crystal and her fellow villagers heard random gunshots a mile or so away one night, they became increasingly concerned – not only for their own wellbeing but especially those of their children.

A few nights later, after Crystal had put the last of her youngsters to bed, she heard a sound outside, and since it was unlikely that anyone from the village would be around at this time she decided to investigate. As she crept outside with a sense of deep trepidation, she could just make out in the darkness the silhouettes of a gang of men moving furtively through the village, speaking to each other in hushed, urgent tones.

In no doubt that these men were there to create damage and havoc, Crystal retreated into her home, woke her children quietly and peered outside to check that the coast was clear. She quickly led her family out, but at that moment the village erupted with the unmistakeable rat-tat-tat of machine gun fire. Chaos ensued, with men, women and children screaming and running in all directions. Some fell as bullets tore into them, and all Crystal could do was flee, gripping tightly onto her children, running blindly, with no idea which direction would lead them to safety.

Suddenly, she noticed a woman, standing completely still perhaps fifty metres in front of her. She thought the woman must be paralysed with fear, but as she drew nearer she recognised that this woman was her grandmother, Nansi. Had it not been for the terror of the moment, Crystal herself might have been rooted to the spot, for Nansi had died many years previously.

Crystal's grandmother now gave a small nod of reassurance and then raised her left arm slowly, pointing with her index finger. As Crystal looked to see where Nansi was pointing, she spotted an opening between the trees of a wooded area and an overwhelming feeling that all would be well came over her. She ran with her children in that direction and kept on running until they collapsed to the ground with exhaustion. As she looked up, her grandmother was there again, this time smiling with such love that her eyes glistened with tears.

Then Nansi spoke briefly. 'Hide, hide,' she urged as she pointed to a thicket of bushes. Crystal again trusted her grandmother's directions and ran towards the thicket, nestling herself and her children deep within its protective foliage. She peered back to the moonlit spot where Nansi had stood, but her grandmother had vanished as suddenly as she had appeared.

Throughout the night, armed renegades continued to ransack the village and surrounding area, on one occasion one of the bandits came so close to where Crystal and her children were hiding that she could see the scars of a previous battle on his face. But he did not see Crystal and despite the loss of many of her friends and neighbours during that terrible night, the story ended happily for her and her children.

Sitting in a coffee house in London's West End, I heard this tale from a student of mine who was telling a group of us about his experiences as an aid worker in the Sudan. When I asked him how Crystal had felt on seeing her grandmother, he said he had also asked her this question. Crystal told him that she believed her grandmother to be an angel of God, sent to save her and her family. Then she smiled at him and said, 'My grandmother loved me more than life itself. Why wouldn't she want to look after me from heaven, just as she did here on Earth?'

I have often recounted this story as I believe it demonstrates perfectly how the spirit world intervenes in times of real crisis and dilemma. But I have also questioned why on this occasion one young woman's grandmother was there to direct her beloved granddaughter to a place of safety, while many other people perished on that fateful night. Did Nansi manifest physically, so that other villagers, had they been in the right place, could have followed her guidance, or was this phenomenon the result of an innate clairvoyant faculty that Crystal had inherited from birth?

The only conclusion I can draw is that some of us here on Earth are more open and sensitive to the inspiration of the other world, whereas those who are more analytically minded might struggle to see or feel anything the spirit people wish to offer. Looking back through our world's history and considering how revelations and visitations were experienced by the prophets of the past, I feel sure that each of these people were sensitive and loving souls, open to the influence of the heavenly realms and prepared to share with those around them the wonderful knowledge they received.

I left the coffee house that day with my head buzzing, not only from the copious amount of caffeine, but also the incredible story of this spirit encounter. It got me thinking about how aware the spirit people are of what goes on here in our world and how much they can influence our lives if we're receptive to their efforts.

This was obviously meant to be a day of memorable events for me, as it just so happened that I was working that afternoon at a college in South Kensington, where I had four clients for one-to-one readings. By the time my third client left, I was feeling a little tired and so was quite relieved when my last client finally sat down opposite me. A pleasant-faced, middle-aged man, he smiled at me and introduced himself as Andrew. I remember closing my eyes and, as usual, calling out in my mind to the other world, 'Come forward, friends, gather close. Who would like to communicate with this gentleman?'

I fully expected Andrew's mother, grandmother, sister or close friend to draw near, yet all I could feel was a man who seemed to belong to a bygone age. I sent up the thought, 'If you are a guide, wait a while, allow his family to come through first.' I waited and as before, all I felt was this same figure. But this time, I was also aware of beautiful colours and textures of landscapes, flowers and trees, and found myself becoming a little confused. A few minutes had passed already and I knew I had to begin the reading for my client.

Almost apologetically, I began telling him about the colours and textures of the visions I was seeing clearly before me. To my surprise, Andrew sat there wide-eyed, his jaw dropped and he was obviously fascinated by this information.

Next, I saw paintbrushes, canvasses and paints being mixed to create new and expressive colours, and then I felt as though I'd been teleported to a room stacked high with beautiful paintings depicting landscapes and water scenes. All these things I described to my sitter, and so the reading progressed. A number of times, I enquired doubtfully of Andrew, 'Am I working in a way that is acceptable to you?' or 'Do you understand this information?' but he was so enthusiastic that I was happy to continue.

Once again, I felt the man from the bygone age draw near and it seemed that he was standing directly behind Andrew. As soon as I became aware of this, Andrew's eyes began to close and his head dropped slightly forward. 'Oh boy,' I thought, 'I've bored him into submission. He's nodded off.'

With that, Andrew sat up straight, his eyes still shut, and then in a flash his face changed before my very eyes, supplanted by the face of the man who stood behind him. This took me by surprise and I was mesmerised. Then as quickly as it came, the face disappeared, as did the spirit man behind Andrew.

Andrew opened his eyes and continued to look at me as if nothing had happened. I must have appeared a little shocked as he asked me if everything was OK. I told him what I'd seen, and his reply was, 'I knew he would show himself.'

Andrew went on to tell me that he believed the spirit of the great artist Claude Monet was very much with him and had been around him since he was a child. I sat there dumbfounded, as much by this revelation as the incredibly powerful vision I'd seen. There has been the odd occasion in my life when I've read for someone and thought, 'This guy has lost the plot,' but what Andrew was telling me sounded entirely genuine.

After a few moments, I closed my eyes again and became strongly aware of the spirit man, hearing his words in my mind, 'It is true. It is I. I am continuing my work.' Bringing the reading to a close, I relayed these words to Andrew, who seemed very happy with our consultation.

Before he left, Andrew took from his bag what he described as 'the smaller pieces'. They were some of the most beautiful paintings I'd ever seen – and I knew just enough about art to recognise that they were very much in the style of Claude Monet.

Andrew explained how he'd set aside a room in his home, filled with paints and canvasses, where he goes at certain times of the day when he feels inspired. He begins to mix various paints, but before he has a chance to finish, he feels his eyes begin to close and his head loll forwards. He is then, in his own words, 'compelled to let him in'. He described to me how his hands move at lightning speed as he paints and even though he is aware of everything that is happening around him, he feels powerless to interfere with the process. And then as quickly as this entranced state arises, it leaves him, and he's alone in his painting room with a beautiful piece of art as his reward.

I was spellbound as I looked at the paintings. Not only were they obviously well composed, but for me there was also a feeling of complete love and sharing emanating from them. I found it a startling revelation of how some spirit people seem able to continue their work here on Earth by identifying individuals who have the capacity and willingness to allow great art, poetry or music to flow through them.

I find it tremendously reassuring to think that those in the other world are prepared to share with us in this way. It certainly reinforces my belief that we are never truly alone; at moments in our lives when we need assistance and comfort, we are surrounded and supported by those who love us. And more than this, it seems the spirit people work through us by actively manipulating our minds and bodies to create something tangible, a real change in the world. Just think of the wealth of spirit knowledge and talent that would be available if we were only open enough to receive it – if we could only sing, write or carry out humanitarian works when inspired by the likes of Maria Callas, Charles Dickens or Mother Teresa.

There are well-documented accounts from the Second World War, and indeed many other major conflicts in history, of angelic beings appearing to those for whom all hope seemed lost and responding to their desperate need for help and guidance. This is equally so in times of peace, when angels have been sighted, for example, at the scenes of horrific accidents, appearing to lend assistance to those open enough to perceive them.

Seeing all life from an advanced perspective, these beautiful, evolved beings – sometimes described as messengers – have a far greater insight into the workings of the human mind than we attain here in our world. They understand in depth our need to possess and to conquer, our inability to see our opponent's point of view and our tendency to recognise the differences in each other rather than the similarities. They carry within them the answers to age-old questions that have troubled man from the beginning of time, and the key to unlocking many of our physical and emotional dilemmas. All knowledge is there, ready to be shared with those following the path to spiritual discovery and enlightenment.

I am sure we are all aware of how difficult it would be for any of us to set about trying to change the world from a negative to a positive space, healing all physical and emotional problems and solving every conflict that one race has with another. But imagine a day, just one day to start us off, where we could not only open up to the philosophies, insights and healings that the angelic people bring to us, but also channel them through to those in our world who remain closed to them. During that day, not one word of hatred would be uttered, not one negative action carried out; it would be a day filled with smiling faces, warm embraces and inspiring words. I like to think we could potentially heal this world of all that ails it.

I know this may sound like a naïve fool's hopeless fantasy, but the point I'm trying to make is that it all starts with us. While talk of healing the world with the angels' assistance might sound fantastical, if we at least concentrate on developing ourselves and reaching a level of attunement with the creative element of the universe, we will be doing all we can to change this world forever.

I believe that we must remind ourselves daily that we are a spirit being, incarnate within this world, recognising that we are intrinsically linked with all living things around us and that we are responsible for every thought we have and every word we speak. We know there is a creative force behind the universe and I am sure many of you already embrace the reality that you are a part of this same force. So why not spend a day reflecting this back to those around you?

Tomorrow morning, when you wake up, try to be mindful of the needs of others for the entire day, also taking moments out to gaze at the beauty that surrounds you. Appreciate the majesty of a mighty oak tree, delight in the lush greenness of the grass at the roadside, stroke an animal or smile at the old lady in the supermarket queue whose fiddling for small change might normally frustrate you. Continue throughout the day to send out thoughts to those who guide you from the other world, asking them to help you to break free from the restrictions of the mind so that you might reach your full spiritual potential.

You can still enjoy a bar of chocolate, catch up with your favourite TV programme and deal with the issues of the day, but if you perform all your daily activities in a more caring, loving and contented way, you will nonetheless be continuing your spiritual evolution.

Many people find that as their spirituality evolves, so does their psychic awareness. One of the first signs of this is often an ability to feel the atmosphere within a building. When in someone's home or place of work, for example, I sometimes find myself bombarded by feelings and emotions that have built up over many years and still subsist within the very plaster and framework of the building. This is why it's easy for some people, when walking into a new environment, to say, 'This place has a wonderful homely feel to it.' But in a different place, despite there being no signs or knowledge of a previous argument or upset, we feel we could cut the atmosphere with a knife. For many of us this ability is innate and if you can develop it into a real skill you will open yourself to some revealing and fascinating experiences. I well remember an occasion when my sensitivities in this respect led to another one of my adventures – a true 'Stockwell special'!

I was spending a few days away with my mum in Amsterdam and we had had a lovely time meandering around the canals, markets and tulip stalls, not to mention enjoying a few good meals and the odd bottle of wine. One day, after yet more sightseeing, we were walking along a street called Prinsengracht when we saw a very long queue of people waiting patiently outside one particular building. Both of us being quite nosy at heart, we went across to investigate and were intrigued to discover that we were standing outside the house where Anne Frank had lived while in hiding from the Nazis during the Second World War.

Needless to say we joined the queue and after a considerable wait were finally admitted to the building. Along with tourists from all over the world, we were fascinated by the furniture and décor of the period, and studied the many black and white photos on display, depicting happier times for Anne and her family. I felt a deep empathy with Anne as I tried to put myself in her position and feel what it must have been like to be cooped up in a relatively small space for all those years, unable to venture outside for fear of discovery.

For a while, I was happily milling around just like any other tourist. It was only when I entered the bedroom that Anne had shared with her sister that the whole event started to take on a very different perspective.

As I gazed down at Anne's spartan, metal-framed bed, made up with sheets and blankets, I felt a sudden jolt to my body and stumbled backwards slightly. Then, there in front of me, as if I was looking at an old sepia photograph, was Anne herself, sitting with her head in her hands. Before I had a chance to glean any more from this vision, it disappeared. I said nothing to my mother, but carried on the tour along with everyone else.

A few minutes later, I found myself climbing a steep staircase, up into another area of the house. As I neared the top, I felt someone pushing me from behind as they tried to get past and I had to hang on tightly to the stair rail to steady myself. I felt a little annoyed that somebody could be so impatient that they couldn't wait for me to reach the top, but as I looked round to see who it was, I realised there was no one there. I stood for a moment, surprised and slightly bewildered. I was used to seeing unusual things, but this was something quite different – I had been physically pushed by someone and then felt their weight right beside me.

There was nothing for it but to venture on, though I remember Mum asking if I was OK when I joined her at the top of the stairs. I told her I was fine and we carried on into a kitchen area at the top of the house. Here, I became aware of a woman bustling around, dressed in plain, old-fashioned clothing. She seemed so real to me that she could have been an actress employed to create the atmosphere of the time, but when I cast my eyes down to the floor I realised I was only seeing half of this woman. Where her feet should have been there was nothing, as though she was suspended in mid-air. She turned and smiled at me. By this time, Mum was standing at my side, and as I looked at her and then back to the apparition, I realised that neither of them seemed to have registered the other.

The moment was broken at this point when a dozen or so Japanese tourists tried to join us in the small kitchen space. The spirit woman simply faded away, leaving Mum and me pinned to the draining board while the latest entrants excitedly explored the room.

We finally managed to see the rest of the house, before moving on to the museum exhibitions in the adjacent building. But I suddenly had an overwhelming feeling that I needed to return to the house, and as Mum seemed quite happy looking at the many photographs of the era on display, I quickly nipped back. I felt compelled to return to the staircase where I'd been pushed to one side, and this time all seemed well as I went up. There was not a soul to be seen, which was unusual given the number of people looking around earlier. I went back down the stairs, stood at the bottom and closed my eyes, whereupon the most extraordinary thing happened.

As before, I had the same feeling of being pushed by someone who was trying to get past me, but instead of looking round, I kept my eyes closed and opened up my awareness. My mind tumbled back to a time over sixty years before and I heard the terrible sound of shouts and screams and army boots thudding against wooden floors. Then, in my mind, I became aware of a vision of Anne running up the stairs, and I felt the terror of the people who had been discovered by the German troopers. That same feeling of being pushed to one side became even stronger and I now saw the culprit – a young soldier, his eyes wide as he revelled in the thrill of the chase, feeling nothing for the poor souls he was about to condemn to a horrific fate.

These feelings of fear and victory swam dizzily in my mind, and once again I had to hold on fast to the stair rail to steady myself. Then I ventured back to the top of the stairs, but I saw no one, either from this world or the next. Drained, I sank to the floor, pressing my back firmly against the cool plaster behind me. I knew that what I was experiencing was a series of reflections of the past – powerful emotions, trapped within the fabric of the building, replaying themselves repeatedly so that any sensitive person might understand everything that had happened in this place. I knew that Anne was now far away from here, spending time with her family in the spirit world – she would have no reason to dwell on in this place of captivity. Yet despite this I couldn't help feeling unsettled by the senses and memories that had flooded my mind.

I sent a thought to the spirit world, requesting a blessing on this building and asking that they do all in their power to ease the negativity that was so prevalent and replace it with positive energy. I sat awestruck as the whole building seemed to light up, as though someone from above had thrown a massive switch. I knew then that my silent prayer had been answered.

As you might imagine, I was profoundly affected by this experience, not least because of the way it reinforced to me that if we request help from the spirit world, they will do their best to assist. This might not always be in the form we expect, but at least if we trust enough to ask, for the benefit of others, the Great Spirit will answer our prayers.

I've heard many people speak of haunted houses, of paranormal investigators or mediums visiting ancient castles and historic monuments, attempting to feel the presence of spirits who still walk there. But it's my experience that what is often deemed to be a spirit in distress, one that chooses to dwell on Earth for all time – a ghost – is nothing of the sort. It is simply a powerful emotion from the past that has stained the fabric and atmosphere of the building and will continue to affect it for many years to come.

Shortly after my mother and I returned from Amsterdam, I was back at home in Essex, seeing clients for private consultations. One of them was an elderly man who introduced himself as Bill. After the usual pleasantries I asked him to take a seat so the reading could commence.

As soon as I closed my eyes, I could see a young serviceman looking back at me. As I described him to Bill, I heard the name Alec being called. Bill became quite emotional after receiving this information and told me that he did indeed know a young serviceman by this name, who had passed many years before. I then received a vision from Alec, and he showed me very clearly the two of them serving in the army together during the Second World War. Again, Bill confirmed this was correct.

As the reading continued, many details of Alec and Bill's time together were offered, including information regarding a pair of black army boots that had been stolen, and a vivid memory of them both dressing up rather like pantomime dames, complete with dense, fake moustaches, to entertain their comrades.

During the course of the reading, I found myself asking Alec how he had died, as this is always an important piece of evidence for the sitter. However, I wasn't remotely prepared for the scene that unfolded before me. It was like something from an epic war film. I could see a partly burned-out building and two young soldiers hunched with their rifles behind mounds of rubble and debris, their boyish faces smeared with blood and dirt. As I looked on the scene, I was overwhelmed by emotion and hastily tried to compose myself without Bill becoming overly concerned. He asked if I was all right and I reassured him. When I described the scene so clearly imprinted in my mind, he said, 'Oh my God, that's completely right. We were in Arnhem together. I can picture exactly what you're seeing.' With that, he leaned forward and took my hands in his. 'What else do you see?' he whispered.

Feeling encouraged by Bill's eagerness to continue, I closed my eyes again and endeavoured to see more for him. In a second, I saw the two young men now running for their lives. I could hear shooting behind them as they raced through bombed-out buildings, and I was aware of the bodies of the fallen lying all around them.

The vision then jumped forward to night-time. I saw the two of them huddled together for security and warmth, Alec asleep while Bill struggled to stay awake, fighting his exhaustion to keep watch. I was dimly aware that I too was now feeling tired, but suddenly I received the most momentous image. It felt as though I'd been struck by a bolt of lightning, shattering the image in my mind and leaving nothing more for me to see than pure white light. My body must have jolted at this point, prompting Bill to enquire, 'What? What did you see?'

I explained everything to him, and when I mentioned the white light, he sat back in his chair in shock. He gazed at me a moment in disbelief and struggled to find the words to go on.

'I saw it too,' he finally said. 'While Alec was sleeping. You're right, I was keeping watch. And then I saw it.' He stopped again and several seconds went by before, suddenly, Bill and I spoke at exactly the same time, our words seeming to meet as they left our mouths. 'An angel,' we said in unison.

It was an extraordinary moment of synchronicity and again we sat in silence for a few seconds, reflecting on the powerful forces at play here. Then Bill said, 'That angel saved my life.'

He went on to explain how, as I had described, he sat that night feeling hungry, scared and alone. They were almost out of ammunition, hadn't eaten for days and the enemy closing in from every direction. All hope seemed lost and while his friend slept, despite not being a man of any great religious conviction, Bill prayed. He prayed that he might see his home again, give his mother a hug, cuddle his baby sister and see the majestic English countryside where he had grown up. As he repeated these urgent prayers, feeling more and more emotional, he was stunned by a brilliant flash of white light in front of him. In that light stood a beautiful young woman who looked on him with deep kindness, her words seeming to fill his very being. 'Leave this place now,' she said. 'Do not look back. Journey one mile east, find a church with no doors and remain there until help arrives.' With that, she disappeared, leaving the two young soldiers alone again.

Waking his friend, Bill tried to describe what he'd seen and told him that they must move and move now. But as far as Alec was concerned, Bill had taken leave of his senses. Alec was having none of it: he had thoughts and plans of his own and believed that to travel in the direction Bill was suggesting would lead them to certain death. The two men were desperately at odds, neither one willing to yield to the other, and at daybreak they took the momentous decision to go their separate ways.

As I looked at Bill, his eyes were blind with tears. Obviously not a man used to such displays of emotion, he apologised and straightened himself. I told him not to worry, that I understood, and then I continued with the reading, the spirit of Alec staying at my side throughout. I concluded by telling Bill, 'Your friend wants you to know that he should have listened to you that night, that he should never have left you.' I had an overwhelming feeling that Alec had perished shortly after this episode. Bill felt so too – he didn't know exactly when or how Alec had died, but learned of his death a while afterwards.

Bill journeyed as advised by the angelic being and was amazed to find the church she described. He hid inside and less than a day passed before he was rescued by Allied troops.

As he stood to leave, thanking me for the time I'd spent with him, he told me, 'I've no fear of dying. I know my family will be there to meet me – and Alec of course. And I know that when that time comes, I'll get to see my angel again.'

Although Bill's experience is not unique, I find it moving and profound, illustrating that in moments of great need, when we earnestly ask or pray for help, if we have the sensitivity to receive we might be blessed with assistance and protection from the other world.

Calling on the spirit world in this way was never more evident than when I met a young girl with her mother, who approached me after a demonstration I'd given in a spiritualist church in Plaistow, east London. The mother asked whether I would be available to go to her home to read for members of her family. I often did this sort of thing and the usual set-up was that I would read for around six people consecutively, each one having a half-hour session. These readings would generally take place in a spare bedroom of my host's home, and although great work had been done in this way, the whole process could be incredibly tiring, depending of course, on the kind of people I was reading for and how seriously they were taking it.

At this particular time I was inundated with requests to give home visits and I was just about to apologise that my diary was full when I caught a look in the young girl's eyes. There was something pleading in her expression and I had a sense that this went beyond the normal level of interest in my work, especially coming from one so young. Instead of turning them down, I asked their names. The mother introduced herself as Jean and her daughter as Sophie, who was about twelve years old with a pleasant, round face and thick dark hair. When the child gave me that look again, despite the pressures on my schedule, I said, 'Here's my phone number. Call me tomorrow and I'll try to give you an early appointment.'

Suffice to say that a couple of weeks later I was waiting outside the front door of a semi-detached house in Upton Park. My arrival was announced not only by my rap of the doorknocker, but also by a cacophony of barking within the house. There was no question that my host was a dog lover.

Jean opened the door and spent the next few chaotic moments attempting to drag dogs of all different shapes and sizes off me. Being a dog enthusiast myself, as two spoiled border terriers at my home in Essex will attest, I quite enjoyed the process – and dogs do seem to have a happy knack of breaking the ice, so it felt as though Jean and I had bonded even before we reached the sitting room.

Once there, I instantly became aware of a change in energy between the hallway and this room. I glanced around, acknowledging a couple of middle-aged women who resembled Jean so closely that the trio reminded me of the Beverley Sisters. In the corner sat a handsome young man of about twenty-five, who stood up and shook my hand assertively, cheerily introducing himself as Mike, Jean's cousin.

As Mike withdrew, I suddenly had an overwhelming feeling of nausea, which fortunately left me as quickly as it came, and then I heard the reassuring chink of cups and saucers as Sophie walked in with a tray of tea and coffee. She looked so pleased to see me she was positively beaming. I noticed she had a cute Miss Piggy clip in her hair and it seemed she'd made a special effort with her appearance that day.

Presently, I was led into a conservatory at the back of the house, where the readings were to take place. The first few went just fine, and then it was Mike's turn. He sat before me and as hard as I tried to make a link for him, nothing came: it felt as though I was facing a brick wall. I apologised and suggested that we try again at the end of the session, which he seemed happy to accept.

When it came to Jean's turn, she asked if Sophie could sit in with her because she was very interested in the subject matter. Normally I would hesitate to allow someone so young to sit in on a one-to-one reading, but there was something about Sophie that I'd really warmed to. Reasoning with myself that this was Jean's reading and Sophie was purely a spectator, just as she was at the public demonstration where we'd met, I agreed to Jean's request.

As soon as I closed my eyes to make a link to the spirit world for Jean, I heard a woman's voice very clearly in my left ear: 'She's in danger.' This was so loud, determined and real that I was startled. I didn't know what to say to Jean: how could I repeat what I'd just heard? But after a brief pause the voice came again, urging this time in a noticeable Welsh accent, 'Help her. Please help her.'

I asked Jean whether she knew a woman from Wales who had passed, and she confirmed that this was most probably her maternal grandmother. I was then in a rather awkward predicament. Did I convey what I'd heard or should I in some way filter the information? I chose the latter, enquiring whether Jean felt under any pressure or fearful of anything in her life at the moment. She looked back at me, puzzled, and shook her head, so I carried on with the reading.

Because of the way Jean's grandmother was coming through to me, I recognised that it would be easier for me to feel the information she wished to relay to me, rather than rely on what I might be able to see or hear. This way of working is called clairsentience and is used by the majority of mediums. It feels as though we are allowing the spirit people's minds to blend with our minds and in so doing we feel clearly everything they wish to convey. As soon as I allowed Jean's grandmother's feelings to enter my mind, I became horribly aware that it was in fact Sophie who was in danger and not Jean. I also felt strongly that the threat to Sophie was posed by someone known to the family. Then, when the same feeling of nausea swept over me again, I knew that Mike was that person.

I was in complete turmoil. If I was worried about telling Jean what I'd first heard, how could I confide something of this magnitude? How would she react and what would the consequences be? And God forbid I was wrong, that I had in some way misinterpreted the information.

I found myself looking at Jean and saying, 'Your grandmother is here and she believes Sophie to be in danger.' Naturally, poor Jean was horrified and asked falteringly what on earth I was talking about. I told her honestly that I wasn't quite sure myself, but I felt it had something to do with her cousin Mike. Jean looked at her daughter, who had been sitting quietly throughout, and as soon as their eyes met, Sophie started to cry.

While Jean took Sophie upstairs to her bedroom, I sat alone in the conservatory, not knowing whether I'd done right or wrong. The house seemed so quiet and I wondered whether I should get up and leave, but then Jean and Sophie came back in and Jean said, 'I've asked Mike to leave.'

I apologised for any upset I might have created. Even though Jean still seemed in a state of shock, she assured me that everything was fine. I collected my things and went to the front door. As I was about to leave Sophie ran towards me and without a word being spoken gave me a big hug. She held out the tiny plastic Miss Piggy clip and pressed it into my hand. 'Thank you,' she said, 'I knew you'd be able to help me.' And then she ran upstairs to her bedroom.

Some weeks passed and I received a letter from Jean describing how a few weeks prior to our meeting Mike had started to show a particular interest in Sophie. He took her to dance classes, to the cinema and on trips in his delivery van when he was working. Jean's only thought at the time was how kind Mike was to look after Sophie, as she had never known her father.

Jean didn't go into detail in her letter, but it was clear from the subtext that Mike had started to act inappropriately towards Sophie, and that she was too scared to say anything. After the sitting, Sophie opened up to her mother. Jean concluded by telling me that she had cut off all communication with Mike and forbidden him to visit her family again.

I couldn't help reflecting on how extraordinary it was that the spirit world had influenced the course of events in this way. They were aware of Sophie's dilemma and wanted so much to protect her that they put forward an intermediary to speak on their behalf. Even though the message was incredibly difficult for me to give, I've learned over many years that sometimes I just have to pass on what I receive, in the hope that it will benefit and enable those who come to me for help.

5
Superstars in the Sky

'We shall find peace. We shall hear the angels, we shall see the sky sparkling with diamonds.'

Anton Chekhov

When I'm working as a medium and bringing through spirit messages, even though it might not always be apparent to those attending, my spirit guide is always present. Most of the time he isn't mentioned or acknowledged and is content to take a back-seat while I stand centre stage. I am never in any doubt that he is there with me, supporting me in my work as I bring through messages from the loved ones of the people in the audience. To all intents and purposes, he is an unsung hero, but there are certain situations when he steps forward to pass on his wisdom to those present in a more direct way. These occasions tend to be few and far between, but when they arise they are very special and exciting.

In the earlier days of my spiritual development, I was invited by a convinced spiritualist to hold a meeting at her home. I pulled into the driveway and was confronted by an imposing late-Victorian house with its original leaded windows. Before I had a chance to step from my car, the front door was flung open, and sailing towards me was a rather oversized middle-aged woman, who was so excited she seemed about to pop. She whisked me into the front hall and when she threw her arms enthusiastically around me from behind, it was a moment or two before I realised that she was trying to help me remove my coat.

With that task accomplished, I took in my surroundings. It felt as though I'd stepped back in time, but I couldn't help noticing the small beads of sweat on my hostess' forehead, and I had to battle to erase thoughts of the movie *Whatever Happened to Baby Jane?* in which Bette Davis played the crazed sister.

The woman explained that she had invited just her closest friends to this auspicious occasion, and then excitedly led me into a front parlour which was lit by the red bulb of a standard lamp. All I could make out were the most obvious features of the room's occupants, and it seemed that a dozen or so noses were sat pointing in my direction.

After a formal introduction by my hostess I was asked to take a seat. The purpose of this particular evening was for me to give an inspirational talk, whereby I would allow myself to enter an altered state of consciousness, during which my own guides would merge with my mind in such a way that their intelligence and thoughts would be expressed through me. It is an incredibly special connection built on mutual trust and willingness to share a space for a few minutes of earthly time. This might sound a little strange to the uninitiated, but this kind of phenomenon is very real indeed.

After a brief request to those assembled to avoid loud noises and sudden movements, to remain in the room and keep conversation to a minimum, I closed my eyes. I began to focus my attention on my breathing, taking slow, deep breaths for a few minutes before addressing the spirit world, my simple but sincere words spoken only in my own mind: 'Welcome friends, gather close to me. Inspire me with your thoughts.'

It is always at this point in a situation like this that I feel something magical happening, and I become incredibly aware of the presence of the other world. I usually feel my own guide first, and this particular evening was no exception. As he came closer to me I started to feel older and my body seemed much smaller than its usual frame. Then I felt my spirit friend's saffron robes being wrapped around me and I also became aware that my blonde hair was replaced by a smooth, bald pate. My heart pounded and my breathing quickened and became shallower. Then, when I felt my throat tighten, I knew that my guide was about to address those assembled.

It was as if I was being compelled to speak. I opened my mouth and words came, not from my own thoughts, but inspired by the feel of my spirit: 'Welcome, my name is Zintar. I am pleased to speak with you. Many of you have come to hear me speak this night, hoping for revelations and information that will lead you to a place of enlightenment. So as I speak with you, do not just open your ears, but open your minds and your hearts also, to allow these spirit truths to echo into the very core of your being. Allow my words to resonate within you, allow me to guide you to a place where all knowledge flows. My name is Zintar. Allow me to speak with you.'

I spoke in this way for over an hour and through each sentence it felt as though I was a member of the audience listening to someone else speaking, sharing in his philosophy and marvelling at his wisdom. I appreciate how difficult this might be to comprehend, but all I can say is that this is the way it is.

Then the words faded away, and as I felt Zintar leaving I started to feel a little more like me. By focusing again on my breathing and trying to move my fingers and toes, I was becoming more grounded and aware of the space in which I sat. As I opened my eyes, I saw those in attendance, sitting so quietly, gazing back at me, and I really wasn't sure what to say or do next. Then the silence was broken as my hostess began to clap energetically. Everyone joined in spontaneously and I breathed a sigh of relief as I realised that they had all enjoyed the session.

It turned out to be a fabulous evening, and two hours and several cups of tea later I was still there, answering question after question about the mechanics of this form of mediumship. Then my hostess led me outside and when we reached my car she enveloped me in a rib-crushing embrace. I felt wonderful, as though I really had been of service to the spirit people during that evening.

In the many years since those early days of my mediumship practice, my relationship with Zintar has developed to the point where I consider him not only my confidant and helper, but one of my greatest friends. The very first time I became aware of him was when I was still a teenager, sitting in a development group run by the late Joan Barham, and he appeared to me in the guise of an ancient Tibetan monk. He showed me a previous lifetime that we had lived together, high in the mountains of Tibet. I've had many intense visions of this life since then, seeing Zintar walking in front of me, a staff in his right hand, his old body hunched forward. I was always following close behind as I was still a child then and Zintar was my master and teacher.

It was during one of these visions that I saw how Zintar and I had died. As we walked the mountain path, I saw boulders and rocks tumbling down the mountainside and I knew that I was going to die in this rockfall; yet I also knew that the event was simply the beginning of a whole new chapter. I couldn't possibly have had any inkling at that time of the connection that would endure between my teacher and myself. We lived together, passed together in that life and have been pulled together in this one; and even though I am here and he is there, he is still my guide and my friend.

I sometimes feel Zintar's powerful influence when I'm doing one-to-one readings, especially when a child comes through for his or her parents. I will see Zintar appear in my mind and know instantly that there is something special to be done here – as though those in the spirit world are going to pull out all the stops to make this reading as good as it can possibly be. Once I can see Zintar, a child will appear at his side. In fact this has happened so often now that even before I see the child I sometimes find myself declaring out loud to my sitter, 'I know you have lost your child. My guide is here. He brings them forward.' This instinct has never let me down.

It was during one such occasion that I found myself explaining to Rachael, a young woman in her late twenties, that my guide was coming close and that with him was her daughter, who wished to say hello. My statement was met by a look of utter astonishment on the young woman's face. She didn't move or make any comment, but just stared at me, her eyes wide with expectancy. I was so confident that the information I was receiving was true that I went on to describe the little girl. I saw clearly that she had lush, dark, shoulder-length hair, an olive complexion and laughing eyes – and I knew that she was just six years old when she passed away. She showed me how her mother had sat cradling her for the last few days of her life and I knew instinctively that this little girl had been allowed to die at home, surrounded by all the things she loved and cherished. She showed me her favourite doll, with its sparkly pink headband, then Eeyore from *Winnie-the-Pooh*, with a tattered left ear. She allowed me to see her bedroom, complete with a princess bed adorned by a fuchsia-pink canopy, and told me, 'This is my bedroom, a big girl's bedroom.'

Only after describing everything I had seen did I finally look to her mother for some kind of response. 'Does this make sense to you?' I asked. The poor woman could barely speak, but nodded her head positively so I continued. 'She shows me clearly the 25th December. I know that's Christmas Day, of course, but does it mean anything else to you?'

I waited a few moments as Rachael gazed unseeingly at the floor, and when at last she met my eyes, the corners of her mouth lifted and she broke into a beautiful smile. 'That's her birthday,' she said, clearly affected by the revelation that her daughter lived on.

I continued with the reading and when our session was almost at an end I asked Rachael, 'Is there anything else you need from your daughter?'

She thought for a while and then said, 'I know that she's here. I can't believe how accurate this has been. But one thing you haven't told me is my daughter's name.'

This took me somewhat by surprise. I had so enjoyed feeling this little girl's personality and passing on her wonderful memories that I hadn't even attempted to bring forward this valuable piece of information. So I closed my eyes again and focused intently to see if I could pick it up. I sat for some time and yet nothing came. When I mentioned the names Jessica, Louise and Kirsty, Rachael told me they were all her daughter's friends. I then received the name Claire in my mind, and although Rachael looked heartened, I had still not told her what she so needed to hear. 'That's her sister's name,' she said.

I found myself becoming enormously frustrated – why on earth could I get her friends' and her sister's names and yet not that of the little girl herself? So I tried a different tack. I visualised the name Claire in my mind and spoke with the other world, repeating in my thoughts, 'Come on little girl, your sister's name is Claire, what's your name?' I asked her to place her name next to her sister's in my mind, and then focused hard. 'Claire and . . .?' I repeated inwardly, each time leaving a space, waiting for the name to drop into it. After a few attempts, I found myself exasperatedly telling Rachael, 'I'm really sorry, I can't feel her name. It's just not coming to my mind.' She was very generous and told me it didn't matter – the essential thing for her was that she knew her daughter had been there during our session.

As she stood to go, I held my hand out to shake hers and she stood on tiptoes to kiss me goodbye. It was then that I felt Zintar's presence by my side and I heard him say, 'Charley.' He spoke with such a feeling of love and joy that I knew this had to mean something to Rachael. I repeated the name to her and she reeled backwards with a gasp. 'That's her. Charley. That's my daughter.'

After Rachael left, I sat for a while, still very much aware of the presence of Zintar by my side. 'Thank you,' I told him. 'Thank you for bringing Charley to her mother.' His response filtered back into my mind, 'This is our work, this is our path.' And then he was gone.

Throughout my life I have derived much pleasure from the messages I've brought, the people I've met and the lives I've been able to touch. Nonetheless, the nature of my work is such that I find myself doing a great deal of travelling, both in this country and abroad. I stay in one hotel after another and even though I'm surrounded by people I sometimes really miss my family and friends. In these moments, I often sense one of my spiritual inspirers gathering close, offering support and encouragement in my work.

A few years ago, I spoke to a good friend of mine – an amazing tarot card reader – about these gentle encounters with my spirit friends, and expressed my sense of frustration that I couldn't know more about their lives in the spirit world or fully converse with them. My friend suggested I should ask my spirit guides to work with me to see whether I might glean a greater understanding of the other world. There are moments in our lives when a sudden realisation hits us straight between the eyes and this was one such occasion – why hadn't this occurred to me before?

So, improbable though it sounds, I set out to do just that. I was taking a day off from work and had some time to spare, so I sent up my thoughts to the spirit world to make them aware of my intentions. It was my great hope that as I entered a sleep state that night, they would join me and show me what their home was like.

As you can imagine, by the time I eventually got to bed I was feeling full of anticipation and hoping like mad that my request would be granted. I closed my eyes and called in my mind to my spirit friends, 'Friends, allow me to join you. Allow me to see your world and know how you live.' And then I waited . . . and waited . . . and waited.

Needless to say, sleep wasn't an option and I spent the next few hours tossing, turning and becoming ever more frustrated that my big moment continued to elude me. I imagined the other world preparing for my visit and wondering why I was late for my appointment. Would they give me another chance? To cut a long story short, that evening I travelled no further than the bathroom and back.

The second night was similar, with the exception that I did at least manage to sleep, so deeply that as I woke up I couldn't even remember any dreams. On the third night, after giving a demonstration in Manchester, I crawled into my bed at a hotel and, with no thoughts other than how tired I was, drifted straight off to sleep.

It must have been in the dead of night that I awoke, feeling most peculiar. My eyes were wide open, my breathing laboured and I knew that I would be unable to move even if I wanted to. I felt weightless and my body was shuddering from head to toe. 'Oh my God,' I thought, 'what's going on?'

And then it happened. I was suddenly aware that the spirit part of me was lifting from my physical body. I looked back and saw myself lying in the hotel bed, and then I sensed that even though I was leaving my physical body behind, I still had a body – two arms, two legs and a head – and it looked exactly the same as the form I was leaving behind. Then, as if powerfully pulled by an unseen force, I found myself hurtling through the building and up into the moonlit sky.

Even though this experience happened in the dead of winter, I didn't feel the cold for a second. Neither did I feel the slightest trace of fear or trepidation – I felt like a bird trapped in a cage for a lifetime and then suddenly liberated. I felt more alive than ever as I looked down at the buildings and cars below, then up at the velvety blackness of the sky, sprinkled with stars that glistened like diamonds. I remember thinking, 'You're free, free at last. Fly higher!'

I suddenly felt myself being pulled further, faster, higher. I've no idea of speeds I was travelling – parts of this journey are now a blur to me – but I saw colours of every hue and experienced an overwhelming sense of love throughout the entire episode.

I don't know how long I journeyed for, but I eventually found myself drawn to a perfect white light, which called to me as if it knew me and wanted me to enter. As I did, the first thing I was aware of was that the light seemed to be alive, with music, feelings and emotions, and I knew that I was entering the spirit world. I had reached my destination.

Now walking rather than flying, I looked down towards my feet and stopped in surprise – I was wearing sandals, whereas when I began my journey I was barefoot. I was even more astounded to note that my body was now clad in a long, orange robe, which seemed to have an extraordinary power of its own, its vibrancy bringing me clarity and energy. I stood for several moments trying to take in every thought, every feeling, every image, knowing I must remember as much of this as I could for when I returned home.

It was then that I heard a voice behind me, 'So, you wanted to join us? You wanted to see our world?' Without looking round, I knew this was the voice of Zintar. I took a moment to compose myself; I could barely believe I was about to come face to face with someone who had meant so much to me for so long. When I finally turned to greet him, there he stood, his posture no longer hunched as it had been in Tibet, his wise, kind eyes gazing into mine and glistening as if he was also moved to see me. He held his arms out towards me and I could feel his emotion as we embraced – a precious moment that will stay with me always.

There was no need for words; we expressed ourselves on a mind-to-mind level. I knew his thoughts, just as he knew mine. We were as one. I felt instinctively that he needed to share something with me, and he led me by the arm to a place I can only describe as a heavenly garden. There was nothing formal about it, rather the spirit of Nature had been given free rein to create the most stunning, intoxicating displays of natural beauty. I looked up and saw extraordinary trees, varieties I had never seen before; I saw flowers in colours infinitely more vibrant than anything you would see on Earth; the air smelled sweet and as it blew gently through the trees, it was as though you could hear them sing.

We stopped and I wondered whether our journey had come to its end. Then my heart leapt as I heard a name spoken, the name of a dear old friend, 'Star.'

While I fully accept and am privileged to have Zintar as my guide, guardian and teacher, there is another who dwells in the other world and plays a special role in my life. I have been aware of Star for some years, but he seems only to visit me from time to time, although each occasion has a major and positive impact on me. I sometimes think of him as my superstar in the sky.

I turned, yet was unprepared for the beauty of the vision that awaited me. Star walked towards me, each step effortless and exquisitely graceful, dressed in a pure white robe that shimmered as if threaded with silver. His seemingly ageless, strikingly handsome features were set off by glossy, chestnut-brown hair and the light in his eyes seemed to dance as he smiled at me with profound kindness. As he came closer, I saw how light streamed from the core of his being, right through to his fingertips, toes, eyes and mouth. I was completely mesmerised as I gazed at the most perfect being I had ever seen.

Moments passed. Again there was no need for spoken words as I knew he could see into the very depths of my being. And then I heard in my mind his simple greeting, 'You know me as Star. I am your guardian angel.'

Although words cannot describe the depth of emotion I experienced in that moment, I felt truly blessed and very, very humble. I turned to Zintar, who remained at my side throughout, and saw that he was smiling too.

All too soon, I felt my entire being start to shudder, just as it had in my hotel room, and I knew that my time in this magnificent place was coming to an end. Although I was sad to leave, I nonetheless felt empowered, for I believed absolutely that I would journey back to the land of the spirit on another occasion in the future.

I seemed to hit the bed with a thump. I was back. But now the bird that had soared freely from its cage a short time before had had its wings clipped.

For days afterwards my thoughts were a muddle; it was difficult to concentrate on anything, for no matter what I tried to do, my mind was consumed by my glorious adventure, my fleeting glimpse of the other world. It was almost overwhelming to know for sure that not only was I watched over by Zintar, but also by the spirit I knew as Star, who had now been revealed to me as an angelic being.

Even when I am totally alone, I never feel lonely – because I know beyond all doubt that both Zintar and Star walk with me. I might not always see, hear or sense them, but when I need them for extra reassurance they are there. This was never more so than on a recent visit to the USA to meet with a number of television production companies.

One of the wonders of television is that people get to see you all over the world, whether your show is screened in a particular country or has been burned onto a disc and sent to family or friends by an avid fan. This is something that has happened with every TV show I have appeared on, and I have been fortunate to receive letters asking for my help from people in countries as diverse as Poland, Argentina and Pakistan. Despite all this, it was still a surprise when I received a telephone call from an American television producer, who happened to be based in London but had contacts with a production company in the USA. She had seen my work here in England and thought it would be a great idea to take my psychic talents to the States.

I had already worked in America, on a one-off special for Living TV, called *Street Psychic in San Francisco*. I'd loved the entire experience – America itself was great, but the people I met were awesome – and nearly everyone I spoke to was hugely enthusiastic when I mentioned that I was a British psychic and had travelled to America to share my spiritual gifts. Each reading I conducted was met by the most incredible reactions: unlike the sometimes more reserved audiences in the UK, people Stateside have no inhibitions about shouting out, 'Oh my God, that's *amazing*!' or, 'How do you *know* that?' Of course, the human part of me lapped up that level of enthusiasm!

So when this latest producer asked me if I'd be prepared to go back to the States for a few meetings with various TV channels, it was an easy decision. To cut a long story short, soon afterwards I found myself being thoroughly spoiled in business class on a flight to Los Angeles. A couple of hours after take-off, having already eaten far too many of the goodies they kept placing before me, I managed to turn down the offer of a choc-ice and felt quite proud of myself for that.

Because my inner child refuses to grow up I am a big fan of cartoons and planned to settle back and watch the movie *Shrek 2*. It must only have been about ten minutes into the film when I heard through my headphones a strange voice, one that clearly didn't belong to a character in the movie. The person speaking was a young lad, quiet at first and then, as if growing in confidence, becoming louder and louder. 'I'm looking for my sister,' he said. 'Speak to my sister. Let her know I'm OK.' This message was repeated two or three times and then faded completely. I felt a little disconcerted, sensing a desperate need in this boy from the other world to be heard – a need for him to relay to his loved ones here in this world that he was indeed a spirit and still very much present. Although I heard nothing more, I was certain I would meet the sister in question and be able to pass on her brother's love.

The rest of my journey passed without incident, although I'm ashamed to say that I did eventually succumb to the temptations of the choc-ice.

I arrived at Los Angeles airport one blisteringly hot summer afternoon. I stood for a moment, a little in awe and a tiny bit intimidated as people jostled, pushed and shoved, all of them talking at twice the volume of any Brit I've ever met.

I was met and escorted to the hotel by a pretty young woman named Karen, who was helping out on the TV project. By the time I got to my room, I felt tired and out of sorts and wondered if, for the first time in my life, I might be succumbing to jet lag. I flopped onto the bed, thinking of the number of meetings that lay ahead and realising that I wasn't at all sure of what was expected of me. I must admit I felt a little bit out of my comfort zone. Had I bitten off more than I could chew? This thought and many more like it scrambled around in my mind until sleep eventually took hold.

The next two days were truly hectic. I was ushered from one studio to another, attending meeting upon meeting with all sorts of colourful characters from networks such as NBC, CNN and ABC, among many others. Each time, I secretly hoped that these television executives would just want to discuss one of the half dozen proposals that were being presented to them. Needless to say, they all wanted me to prove myself by giving either themselves or a colleague a personal one-to-one reading. All I can say is that the spirit people must have really wanted me to do well in the States because they did me proud in every reading I did. By the end of the first day, I was having a ball.

On the second day, a meeting that had been arranged at the last minute took place with MTV. I was initially confused, thinking they dealt only with music-related programmes, but then I was reminded that they had also produced a host of reality-based shows.

I was led into their rather trendy offices and met by one of the executive producers and her assistant. As soon as the meeting was under way, I couldn't help feel a wave of cynicism emanating from the producer. As Karen outlined to her the prospective show and its content, I noticed the producer's lips begin to twitch as though she were trying to suppress an outburst of laughter. I began to wonder whether this meeting had been arranged at the last moment simply for its comedy value, but on a more serious note I was becoming increasingly frustrated by her closed-minded attitude. Eventually, I decided I had two options. One was to leave, the other to show her what I could do. In this particular case, I definitely favoured the former, but before I could do anything about it, my mouth had disengaged from my brain and the latter offer made.

The producer's expression was a satisfying mix of disbelief and shock, with possibly a touch of fear thrown in for good measure. Then she immediately looked to her hapless assistant and said to me, 'Do her.'

And so I did.

The reading commenced in the normal manner. I closed my eyes and visualised the young woman in front of me and called in my mind to the spirit world. I instantly sensed that my guide Zintar was there beside me and as soon as I knew this I felt safe. I then became aware of the presence of an elderly lady and could feel her strong, noble character and deeply religious convictions – she was definitely a force to be reckoned with. I clarified with the young woman that this was her maternal grandmother and went on to offer some evidence and personal memories, all of which she accepted as accurate.

I then opened my eyes, thinking that the reading was finished, but when I looked at my sitter, there was something about her expression that made me feel I hadn't completely satisfied her need to receive. So once again I closed my eyes and focused intently. As soon as I did, I felt Zintar once more at my side, and with his presence came the memory of the boy who had spoken to me on the plane a couple of days before.

I opened my eyes and looked directly at the young woman. 'You have a brother in the spirit world,' I told her. Immediately, her eyes welled with tears. 'He was still very young when he passed,' I added, and then saw in my mind's eye the number thirteen. As soon as I mentioned this to her, she began to cry. I went on to describe a feeling of tightness in my chest and her brother's memory of being unable to breathe properly. No sooner had these words left my mouth than I clearly saw a young boy walking down a street and suddenly collapsing. I felt the emergency services trying to resuscitate him and I knew that he had passed suddenly of heart failure, brought on by a severe asthma attack.

All these details I recounted to his sister, also imparting personal memories and more and more information that could only have come from her brother in the other world. 'He knows you have struggled massively with his death,' I told her, 'but he needs you to know that he will always love you and will forever be not only your brother but also your guardian angel looking over you.'

By the time I finished this contact, the atmosphere in the room had changed. The poor young girl who had sat for the reading more out of a sense of duty than desire looked completely different. She had dried her tears and was smiling and happy. She said she felt lighter and brighter. The biggest transformation of all, however, was in her boss, the cynical TV producer, who seemed beside herself as she tried to high

Superstars in the Sky

five in the air. 'God, man,' she said, 'that was out of this world.'

And, do you know, she was right.

All in all, America was a great success. Discussions continue with regard to different projects there and I have a strong feeling that the spirit people are intent on getting the message out to a wider group of people – and will keep doing everything in their power to make their voices heard.

I find the very thought that the spirit people have minds of their own and ambitions to achieve completely fascinating. Sometimes, for example, I might find myself saying within a message, 'Your mother has been waiting some time to communicate with you,' or 'Your father needs to ask for your forgiveness.' Or it might be that a husband who has just passed to the other world is anxious to talk to his wife about an insurance policy. The spirit people do not only want to speak with us to advise us of their survival after death; for them life continues in much the same way as it did here on Earth. They still feel the need to participate in our lives, such as attending the forthcoming marriage of a beloved granddaughter, talking to us about any concerns we may have and sharing in our laughter.

I have given many messages over the past twenty or so years that often seem odd. Just the other day, I was asked to remind a woman in the audience at a theatre demonstration that she and her father had cooked and eaten a hedgehog together! At the same demonstration, a young man returned to his mother and sister to tell them that it didn't matter that they were stuck in traffic and unable to be with him in his dying moments.

I've often thought that within the practice of mediumship there is always a certain element of tug-of-war taking place between the medium and the spirit people. This might sound

107

a little confusing, but the medium has a need to prove that the spirit person exists and so always seeks evidential statements from them – for example, identifying their name, age when they passed, physical description, occupation and unique facets of their personality. Without such evidence, the recipient would be clueless as to who was coming through and it would be very difficult for the medium to pass on messages of love.

When the spirit people come close their main objective is not to bring such statements, but rather to speak in a far more poignant and personal way, such as, 'I have been watching over you since I've been here. I saw the baby born – isn't she beautiful? Dad's here and your nan – we're all here looking at you now. We went with you on holiday too. You should remember to put a higher sun factor on your shoulders – you know how you burn.' All this is lovely, but it could easily relate to more than one recipient in the audience.

So you can see that what makes a good message is a blend of the two. Ideally, there will strong opening evidential statements, such as, 'I have your mother here. I know she was seventy-four years of age when she passed. She talks of her sister Dorothy. I know she worked in a factory and had nine children.' When these crucial statements have been claimed by a willing recipient, the medium can then relax into bringing a fuller expression of what the spirit people wish to convey.

Every now and then, I will have a sitter who comes in with a very specific list of requirements, and over the years there have certainly been times when no matter what I've said it's not been quite enough. Only when I've nearly completed the consultation will they tell me something like, 'Dad and I had a prearranged code word that he has to say before I can believe that he is still with me' or, 'My mother had a special nickname for me that only she would know and unless you can tell me this I will never believe.'

Well, talk about pressure! You'd think it would be enough to describe accurately the people who come forward and give evidence that would bowl over most recipients, but no, some want the combination to grandma's safe. I'm not saying that it's impossible to receive such cryptic information, just that it might pickle the medium's brain in the process.

I'm reminded of my first such experience many years ago, when I was invited to give a group reading to a family in grief. The appointment was scheduled for a weekday evening, which meant I would have to travel from work in London back home to Essex, with just enough time for a quick shower but no dinner.

Chugging along in my old Renault Clio, I finally arrived at an enormous block of flats in Tilbury, Essex. The entrance hall was gloomy, the lift didn't work and unfortunately my clients lived on the twenty-something floor. Desperately trying to catch my breath after an epic climb, and feeling like I needed another shower, I knocked on the door to the flat. It was opened with great eagerness by my hostess, a casually-dressed, dark-haired woman in her forties, who led me through to the lounge and introduced me to her family. After a few pleasantries, I sat down to begin the reading.

As soon as I closed my eyes, I became aware of an eighty-year-old mother who had just passed to the spirit world. This first statement was readily accepted by those assembled. It later transpired that they were all her offspring. I detailed how she passed and how she looked, even down to the fact that she had dyed her hair jet-black up until the time she passed. I described her looped earrings and her love of scarves of every colour. I went on to mention her fascination with Elvis Presley, whereupon her children declared, 'That's Mum all right. She was crazy about him – she always wanted to go to Memphis.' Then I received a clairvoyant image of the name 'Eleanora'. This was met by howls of excitement, confirming, 'You've got it, that's Mum's name! '

I was now feeling pretty good about myself. 'I've nailed it,' I thought triumphantly. As I brought the reading to an end, I fully anticipated a huge round of applause, but my expectant gaze was met only by a succession of blank looks. A heavy air of disappointment hung in the air for a few moments, then they all seemed to say in unison, 'What's the password?'

'The password?' I thought. 'What on earth are they talking about?'

I sat in disbelief as they explained to me that their mother had told them that when she died, if there was indeed an afterlife she would come back with a particular password. I felt completely stumped and had no idea how I might receive such information. But I was young, with an earnest desire to please, and so I closed my eyes and practically begged the other world to reveal to me the magic word. I tried and tried, and if it's possible to squeeze the brain dry I think I managed it that night. Whatever image came to mind, I tried valiantly to explore it and at one point found myself attempting to identify the hidden meaning behind a bunch of daisies. I thought that they might represent a reference to the song about a 'bicycle made for two', but each line of enquiry I pursued was met only by glum faces.

I was on the brink of giving up and admitting failure when it was suggested that I might get a stronger connection with their mother if I held something that belonged to her. Well, I'm not making it up when I say that from a dusty corner cupboard her family retrieved and offered up her false leg. What I was supposed to do with this wasn't immediately apparent, but I accepted it graciously and placed it gently on my lap. Again I closed my eyes, hoping that connecting with something so tangible would invoke a stronger sense of what I was supposed to provide.

This time I received a strong impression of Southend sea front. I described the cockle stalls, the deck chairs, the pebbled beach and the waves – but alas no success. With that, I was handed a photograph of the deceased. There, smiling back at me was a happy, round woman, with perfect dimples in her cheeks, and I felt encouraged by the lovely expression on her face. I think it must have been the kindness in her eyes that made me think, 'One last chance, Eleanora. If you can remember the password, for pity's sake let me have it.' I then pleaded for Zintar to help me – in fact I practically begged him, so great was my need to get this information for them.

Then the strangest thing began to happen. For a moment I felt as though I had left the room and transported myself to Southend sea front. Standing directly opposite the theme park there, as though I was looking at everything in sepia tones, I found myself reading the sign above me: 'Peter Pan's Funfair'.

'Eureka,' I thought, as I returned to everyday consciousness. I opened my eyes and surveyed the assembled group, who by this time were perched on the edge of their seats. I couldn't wait to make my big announcement. 'The password is "funfair",' I told them grandly. One or two of them groaned and then my hostess smiled as she looked me squarely in the eye and said, 'No, it's not. Sorry.'

My brain now completely addled, my first instinct was to give up and leave, but as I was about to make my excuses and do just that, a rather obvious thought popped into what was left of my mind. I took a deep breath and proclaimed the words, 'Peter Pan.'

Well, it was as if everyone in the room were experiencing birthdays, Christmas and New Year's Eve all at once. There was now no doubt in their minds that their mother lived on. I sent up a deeply grateful thought to Zintar and was convinced that by way of reply I could hear him laughing at me.

I love recounting this memory, not just because of the power of the connection I had with Eleanora, but also for the way it illustrates the lengths a medium sometimes has to go – with the support of the spirit world of course – before a sitter will believe that we do indeed live on after death.

In a way, we're all searching for something. Whatever that may be is of course unique to us and will depend on our life's experiences – whether we have lost someone we loved or are yearning for a greater truth to help us successfully navigate a course through life. Of all the thousands of one-to-one readings I've given to date, most have involved communication from the other world, but some have focused on aspects of the sitter's life, where information is received on a psychic level and involves no spirit input. It comes easily to my mind in relation to someone's life, for example, their career aspirations, relationships, financial status or wildest dreams. This for me is an intriguing facet of my work. To know things about an individual and be in a trusted position to advise and guide is something I regard as a great privilege.

But there is another aspect of my work, possibly the least well known, that I call reading on a soul-to-soul level. Some clients will seek my guidance, often after they have already received evidence of a life after death, because they have a deep yearning to discover and understand more about who they really are. I don't mean physically, of course, but rather that they have a need to uncover the truth about themselves as a spirit being.

Whenever I'm approached by people looking for a deeper meaning in this way, I prefer to read for them while entranced. This allows those from the other world to speak to the sitter through me, so that more direct results are achieved. I'm the first to admit that all this trance stuff sounds far-fetched, but believe me, it's very real. To the casual observer it looks like some weird bloke putting on a funny voice, but genuine trance work can produce a very powerful link to the other world.

To prepare for such work, where possible I will sit in a candle-lit room, burn incense and play potent music involving mantras. I'm sure this is not necessary for the spirit world, but it helps me to get into the right frame of mind. I invite the sitter to take a seat opposite me and place their hands in mine. I then begin a process of allowing Zintar to merge with my mind, and before too long I'm aware of him speaking to my sitter.

When I first began to work in this way, Zintar would invite some sitters to ask questions such as, 'How can I become a better medium?' or, 'What should I do in life to become more spiritual?' Zintar would then answer, providing insight and guidance from his own perspective. We worked together like this for some years, but then everything changed one day when a woman called Sylvia came from Switzerland for a reading.

She sat opposite me in the usual manner and when I felt Zintar come close I sat in readiness, waiting for him to address Sylvia. Suddenly, he seemed to withdraw and in his place came another. I immediately felt I was floating on air and I saw white light, not only all around me but also emanating from within my being. My hands felt as though they no longer belonged to me, my heart raced with anticipation and then from my mouth I heard a commanding voice declare to Sylvia that Star had come to speak with her.

For a moment I was in turmoil. What on earth was happening? I wasn't used to this. I struggled for a second or two to settle my emotions, and then clearly and powerfully more words came, this time just into my mind. 'Trust. All will be well.' I understood from this that Star was going to continue to speak through me. This had never happened before and I have to say it felt wonderful.

Star asked nothing of Sylvia, but instead chose to tell her the reason she had come. 'Your daughter has passed,' he said. 'She is here with us now.'

I heard Sylvia begin to weep, but from this point on there is much I can't recall. I felt transported to another room, and while I vaguely sensed what was being conveyed, I was little more than an eavesdropper on a private conversation.

I became more aware of the words that were being spoken a little later. Star was telling Sylvia that she had once lived an incarnation as a nurse in France and that she and her daughter from the present incarnation had lived that life together. He gave both their names from that time and talked of them as twin souls who repeatedly chose to incarnate together. This is why Sylvia had felt so incredibly lost since her daughter had passed. It was as if she was walking the Earth separated from her soul mate.

The final message came as Star told her something her daughter had done on the night after she died. 'She kissed you one last time,' he said, 'after she had returned to us.'

Star stood to one side and I felt myself becoming aware of my surroundings. I was completely elated as this had been such a wonderful connection with my guardian angel; I felt as though I knew him and that he was as real to me as I was to myself. I managed to contain my excitement sufficiently to enquire whether Sylvia was all right. At first, all she could do was nod, obviously moved, not only by the message she had received, but by the nature of the whole experience.

After a few moments she told me, 'It felt like I was in a holy place. The love as he spoke seemed to fill a space inside me that had been empty for so long.'

As I looked at her, I realised she appeared years younger than the woman who had walked in through the door an hour before. She embraced me and thanked me for her connection, but as she was leaving she turned back, saying, 'Can I just explain something – about my daughter kissing me after she died?' She went on to describe how her daughter had died at only thirty, leaving behind a three-year-old daughter of her own. So bereft was Sylvia that she had taken her granddaughter into her own bed so they could sleep together for comfort.

'She went straight to sleep,' she said, 'although I just lay there, trying to stifle the sound of my weeping. I was willing my daughter to appear to me, and then the strangest thing happened.'

Sylvia described how her granddaughter had suddenly sat up in bed, her eyes still shut, then turned to her and kissed her softly on the cheek. As she did, she said, 'For you, Mum,' and then she lay down again as though nothing had happened. She didn't call Sylvia 'Grandma', as she usually did, but 'Mum', and she was obviously still asleep.

'I've wondered about this for so long,' Sylvia told me. 'But now I know from your guide that it really was my daughter who kissed me that one last time.'

Since then, Star has returned in this way on a few special occasions. When he comes, in addition to more personal communications, there is always a deep and powerful message for the sitter about who they are, why they are here and what they need to do for their own soul to progress. There is always a philosophical leaning to the messages he imparts, and frequently cryptic meanings for the sitter to unravel. But perhaps most uplifting of all is that he gives them an insight into their development potential, no doubt in the hope of freeing the spirit within, to become all that it can be while here on this side of life.

6
Twinkle, Twinkle, Little Stars

'When a child dies, an angel comes down from heaven, takes the child in its arms . . . and visits all the places that had been particularly dear to the child.'

Hans Christian Andersen

One of the best-known and loved songs of all time must surely be 'Somewhere Over the Rainbow', which was written for the 1939 movie *The Wizard of Oz* and originally sung by the film's star Judy Garland. It's a song I was captivated by when I was a child, and it seems apt to mention it now, in this chapter devoted to children.

The first few lines have a particular resonance for me because I also believe in another land, way up high, but in my case it's a heavenly playground where the dreams children dare to dream really do come true. It's a place in the other world for all the children of our world who pass before us – a magical place of lush green grass, heavily-laden fruit trees and perpetual sunshine, where the children are free to run, play and explore as they wish. I've often seen this land in visions and it always seems to me to contain all the things of fairy tales; children come here and have the most marvellous adventures and are as safe and secure as they are when being nurtured and loved in the bosom of their spirit family.

Unless we have been through the harrowing ordeal of losing a child ourselves, it is extremely difficult for any of us to understand the feeling of utter devastation the parents experience. The particular kind of grief that accompanies it is unique compared with any other form of loss. While the grief of losing a parent is terrible, there is nonetheless a certain sense that destiny is unfolding as it should – it seems logical that we should see our parents out before we depart ourselves. But whenever I meet bereaved parents, and sadly this happens all too often, it doesn't seem to matter whether they come to me directly after their bereavement or have lost their children many years before, I still pick up that same, unique sense of loss. It's a feeling I've come to recognise easily, and whenever I sense it I know that these grieving people desperately need to receive a connection with their child.

Sometimes, part-way through a public demonstration, I will look out into the sea of faces gazing back at me and feel a special pull towards certain people, at which point I will quietly ask Zintar or Star whether they might bring through any spirit children. It's not as though the people in the audience suddenly become bathed in pure white light or that I see those from the other world standing with them, it's far more subtle but still incredibly real. There is something within a person's aura that begins to attract my attention, and sometimes this feeling is so strong that I will point them out directly, before even feeling the presence of the spirit world. I will make a very bold statement, such as, 'Can I come to the man at the back in the striped T-shirt. I know you have lost your child.'

I've taken a huge leap of faith in making such a statement, but as the energy surrounding a bereaved parent is hard to miss, it almost always turns out that my intuition was correct. When I hear the audience member confirming the tragic reality of their loss, it's as though something magical happens – the spirit world immediately gathers close, as if drawn in and eager to respond to the recipient's need to receive information. Although I'm still very much in the room or on the theatre stage, I sometimes feel a part of me has entered the spirit world – and this only happens when young children are coming through. I can't help thinking that the spirit people believe that communication from spirit children is of special importance, and I feel they pull out all the stops. They take me over, knowing they will impress their messages more strongly and clearly if my own thoughts are effectively out of the way. I've learned over the years that I get the best results when I just let go of all logic and try not to interfere with the process, and I surrender totally to the thoughts, feelings and impressions that the spirits wish to bring to me.

This approach was never put to better use than at a demonstration I gave in northern Germany, with some help from an interpreter! A little way through the evening, I became aware of a group of spirit children gathering close to me, and so I looked into the audience and told them I was being urged to share with them that three children from the other world wished to communicate.

Almost immediately, a woman at the back of the hall seemed to shine out at me like a beacon. This wasn't a physical phenomenon, of course, but from the impact she had on my mind it might as well have been. As I pointed to the woman, asking whether I might speak with her, I saw her face transformed by shock. I said gently, 'I know you have a child in the spirit world.' As soon as this information was relayed to her by my interpreter, the response came back, 'Yes, that's true.'

You could have heard a pin drop in the audience, yet despite their silence I felt the anticipation mounting as I continued the message. It later turned out that many members of the audience knew the woman in question and were aware of her recent loss. This increased level of attention created an almost tangible energy for me to work in, which seemed to intensify the communication that followed.

I described a young boy, who I sensed was around ten or eleven. The woman responded that he was two weeks short of his eleventh birthday when he passed. I went on to describe his cheeky grin and infectious laugh, and then picked up that he was a very intelligent boy, top of his class at school and with a real gift for languages. All of this the mother agreed with enthusiastically. I then saw a very clear mental image of their family home and knew there was something important to be mentioned about a wooden staircase that seemed altogether too small. This perplexed me for a moment or two, but not wishing to interfere or put my own interpretation on the message, I described what I saw to my recipient.

At this point she showed the first sign of emotion in her voice. Apparently the small staircase led to her son's 'secret' den in the attic, built for him by his father, who was a keen carpenter. As soon as I heard this reference to the boy's den, my mind shot forward and I was there in the den, being urged by the boy to talk about his favourite space.

I then saw, suspended from the varnished roof joists by a fishing line, a series of globes depicting the Earth, Mars, Saturn and the Sun. When I described them to the audience, there was an obvious reaction. Apparently the young boy had been a keen astronomer, and this was a key piece of information, helping so many people that evening to recognise that this was most definitely the boy they knew.

I was now feeling heady, as though swimming in an intense, powerful energy brought forth not only by the other world but created here in the room by the living. It seemed to intensify the link with the other world because, suddenly, as loud as any voice I've ever heard, the name Peter was shouted into my left ear. As soon as I relayed this, the boy's mother leapt up from her seat. She was animated, very emotional and desperate to hear more of her son.

I described how the boy had passed very quickly as a result of having fallen outdoors. I almost didn't need to hear her response because the feelings I was getting were so strong that I knew the information was correct. Asking Peter for a clearer sense of what exactly had happened, I was a little frustrated and disappointed when no further clarification came. Peter obviously had more important things he wanted to say.

'He's talking about a forthcoming baby,' I said to the mother. 'Do you know anyone who's expecting?'

As soon as these words left my mouth, I knew instinctively that it was Peter's mother who was to have another child – and sure enough she admitted that she was three months pregnant. Peter impressed on me how he was looking forward to seeing his new brother and asked me to advise his mother that he would act as guardian angel to the baby and do his best to protect and look after him.

She was delighted to know that Peter was aware of the forthcoming new arrival, but puzzled how I knew she was having a little boy. I reassured her that this was what Peter was telling me and she seemed extremely pleased.

But this was not the end of the message. As Peter continued to give me information, I said to his mother, 'Your son wants you to know that he is now with your father, who is looking after him.' With this, she seemed overcome with emotion, explaining that her father had passed only a week after her son. I felt Peter had more to say, and sure enough he showed me a school exercise book. I saw that it was blue and knew that it contained work relating to a science subject. As I told the mother, she leaned down and pulled out of her bag the exact same blue exercise book. She had found it earlier that day while sorting out some drawers at home and thought she might bring it with her in the hope that it would help Peter to come through.

Finally, I knew the reading was coming to an end. Just as the last messages of love and reassurance were being given, Peter's mother asked me a question. She wanted to know if I could tell her what she kept under her pillow and had slept with every night since her son had passed. I asked the same question of the spirit world and waited for the answer to pop into my mind. I became aware that, whatever it was, it was rolled up into a ball, which Peter's mother happily confirmed. I knew that this ball was soft and black and I became further aware of her holding it in her hands at night when she couldn't sleep. But no matter how hard I tried I couldn't work out exactly what it was. Even so, the mother seemed content that I had given enough of a description. Curiosity took the better of me and I asked her to explain to the audience what the item was. It was a pair of Peter's black woollen socks, rolled up together. There was rapturous applause from the audience, and feeling confident that those in the other world were really looking after me that evening, I moved on with the demonstration.

As I endeavoured to feel the spirit people next to me, I became more aware of the two remaining children – of the original group of three – waiting by my side. I felt touched by this, as if they were standing by, patiently watching and hoping that I would soon concentrate my thoughts on them, which of course I then did. I looked out to the audience and tried to feel where I might find my next recipient, but as I gazed around I became a little confused. There were at least ten people I felt I wanted to speak to, all seated randomly around the room.

In such circumstances it was obviously out of the question to go straight to a recipient, so I started to describe what

I was feeling. I concentrated all my thoughts on the spirit world, asking, 'Who would like to come through first?' To my surprise both the waiting children came forward simultaneously. They were very pretty little blonde-haired girls, one of around seven, the other most emphatically telling me that she was exactly four when she had passed. I sensed they were sisters and that they had passed together, but as soon as I described this to the audience at least a dozen hands went up in the air. 'Oh God,' I thought, 'how on earth is this going to work? How can so many people have lost children in this way?'

It soon became apparent that the girls' entire family had come along to the demonstration, each choosing to sit separately in the hope that it might increase their chances of getting a contact. I asked who the parents were, and in the centre of the front row, right under my nose, the mother stood up, immediately followed by her husband, who was sitting four or five rows back. I asked them to clarify the girls' ages when they had passed, and was told that their elder daughter was eight, and not seven as I had thought, and the younger was exactly four, just as she had so eagerly told me.

For the duration of the contact that followed, I kept my eyes resolutely closed. I don't know why I sometimes do this, but it feels that with some spirit contacts I have to close my eyes to focus fully and get it right.

As soon as I closed my eyes, I became aware of thick, acrid smoke and then saw a house ablaze. With a profound sense of sadness I went on to explain how I believed that the two little girls had died together in this fire. I could hear the mother and father crying in the audience, accompanied by various relatives scattered around the room. When I said that I felt the girls had not long passed, probably within the last year, I was told they died six months ago.

I was getting a strong feeling that the parents of these two sisters were wracked with guilt, torturing themselves over whether they might have done anything differently to avoid such a tragic outcome. Yet the sense I was getting from the other world was that the fire was nothing more than a terrible accident and that the parents had done all they could in the circumstances. It felt important to make this point to them, and they seemed to take a little comfort from it. When I talked to various family members afterwards, they confirmed that the fire was considered by the authorities to be accidental and the cause most likely an electrical fault nobody could have anticipated.

Continuing with the demonstration, the young sisters stayed with me as thoughts of the fire dissipated, leaving me with the sense of the two of them playing around me, laughing and squealing as they chased each other back and forth. At first it seemed it would be too obvious to suggest that the girls were now playing so happily together, but as nothing else was coming to me I felt I should describe what I was seeing. This time their mother responded that the girls had an extraordinarily close relationship, always singing, dancing and playing make-believe together. They were inseparable and she was delighted to think of them carrying on in this way in the other world.

Next, I heard the word 'Ute' being called, and since I've worked in Germany a number of times over the years I knew this to be a female name. When I mentioned it, to my surprise the mother confirmed that this was her own name. I felt pleased that throughout this contact the communication from the other world had been so clear and detailed, but it now felt as though I had brought this family everything I could. Thanking them for their attention and for working with me, I was about to move on when the girls' father spoke out. 'Please continue,' he urged. 'Don't stop, I have a question.'

He then asked in a voice heavy with emotion, 'Please, please, can you tell me, are my daughters happy?' He choked a little as he added, 'Are they pretty again?'

As I heard this, I felt a lump in my throat and had to take a moment to keep my composure. I also felt humbled, realising that I'm often so focused on bringing evidence that I sometimes forget to share simple and basic pieces of information that can be of such reassurance for the grieving. I focused on the sisters' faces and assured their father that they were indeed beautiful. The elder girl then stepped closer to me, indicating that even the old, centimetre-long scar on the right-hand side of her forehead had disappeared in the other world. When I conveyed this to her father, he remembered how she had cut her forehead falling from a swing at a very young age, and he seemed amazed that there was no longer any trace of the scar.

The girls resumed their games and laughter, and I concluded the message by again reassuring the parents that their children were happy and that they would see them again one day.

After I brought the demonstration to a close, there was a long line of people waiting to speak to me and ask questions, many of whom were very affected by the links with the three children who had come through. They all commented on the huge difference these messages would make to the children's families, and even though the majority of them had never experienced the loss of a child, they were deeply touched by what they had witnessed.

Not long after that demonstration, I received a letter from the parents of the two girls. Translated into English by the interpreter who had assisted me, the letter said that after losing their girls, the parents thought they would die from grief. But through the message I passed on to them, they were now feeling a little stronger with each day. 'We know our girls live on,' they wrote, 'and that we will all be together again one day. We can only thank you for what you have done.' I'm always so touched to receive letters like this and to know that the spirits have brought through sufficient evidence to make a real difference to the lives of those who remain, for the time being at least, here in this world.

Thinking about the grief of parents who lose children, I'm reminded of an experience some years ago that took me by surprise and taught me an important lesson. After giving a demonstration in a small spiritualist church near Worthing on the south coast of England, I was approached by a colour-fully-dressed, vivacious woman in her early forties, who asked if I might be available for a one-to-one sitting. When I tried to explain that unfortunately my schedule didn't at that time allow for private work because I was always on the road demonstrating, she cut me short, saying it really was very important. I again politely made my apologies, but as I was about to move on she tried another tack. She said a friend of hers was in desperate need of a reading and if I could come to her home that evening to meet this woman, she would cook me the nicest dinner I had ever had.

Though I was quite peckish by this time, I was also very tired and did my best to explain that I had a very early start the next morning and must decline the kind offer. Undeterred, she placed a hand on my arm and said pleadingly, 'She lost her daughter last week.' As soon as I heard this my heart melted and I agreed to see her friend, adding that my time was limited and I would reluctantly have to forego dinner.

Twenty minutes or so later, I was ushered into a smart, terraced house. 'She's in the conservatory,' my hostess said softly and led me into the open-plan living space. Sitting in an armchair in the conservatory was an elderly woman. I stopped in my tracks, thinking she either looked a lot older than her years or had somehow had a child extremely late in life. But deep down I knew that neither option was plausible and turned to my hostess, confused. 'I thought you said—'

'What, that she had lost a child?' she smiled. 'She has.' And then ribbing me gently, she added, 'It may not have been a small child, but I don't think that matters any less, does it?'

I hastily agreed that of course it didn't, then she took me through to meet her friend, Valerie, whose smile as we were introduced did little to conceal the expression of profound grief in her eyes.

I sat down opposite Valerie and tuned into the other world, almost immediately becoming aware of a spirit woman who I instinctively knew was the 'child' in question. I felt she was in her early forties and had passed from cancer. As soon as I mentioned this to Valerie she became emotional, unable to speak but nodding her head to confirm that this information was correct. I told her I knew she had held her daughter's hand as she passed. Then I saw a large letter K in my head, which was so clear that I suggested her daughter's name might be Karen or Kim. Valerie confirmed I was on the right lines, but that the name was in fact Kay. I kicked myself for having let my thoughts jump ahead to possible names – why hadn't I just said 'K'?

Apart from that the reading went very well, with many strong evidential statements. Then, towards the end of the contact, Kay mentioned her love for her dog. I could see in my mind that it was a Cavalier King Charles Spaniel, and Valerie confirmed that she was now looking after her daughter's dog in her own home. Kay's thoughts ran through my head, 'Ask my mum to love my dog and give him loads of kisses.'

Valerie almost broke down completely when she heard this, and confessed to allowing the dog to sleep on her bed.

'The funny thing is,' she told me, 'I don't even like dogs. I only do it because Kay loved him so much.' She went on to describe how she sometimes found the dog's behaviour strange. He would sit by the door, or on the bed at night, howling. I then received a strong impression from Kay that her dog sensed her presence whenever she was around, and I told Valerie that this behaviour, which seemed bizarre to her, was in fact an indication that her daughter was right there in the room with her. I can still picture the look of amazement on her face.

As I brought the message to a close, I felt compelled to look down at Valerie's hands, where I saw a wedding band and solitaire-diamond engagement ring. I had a powerful sense that this engagement ring had belonged to Kay, which Valerie confirmed, explaining with a wry smile, 'When Kay's boyfriend left her, she wasn't about to part with his ring as well. Then when she knew she wasn't going to get better, she gave it to me.'

Feeling the connection coming to an end, I became aware of the lateness of the hour and the journey I still had to make home. I made my apologies and stood up to leave. Valerie gave me a big hug and a squeeze, impressing me with her strength. 'Thank you for bringing me my baby back, my little girl,' she told me.

I have to confess that my hostess was right to chastise me a little when we arrived, because I really had agreed to come to this house believing I'd be reading for the bereaved mother of a small child, as if in some way that was more important or urgent. Yet I only properly understood for the first time that night that the grief of all those who have lost a child is exactly the same. Age doesn't enter into it – the love that exists between a parent and child is continuous and everlasting, even beyond the grave.

Perhaps because a part of me refuses to grow up, I've always loved children; but it's only recently that I've come to understand fully the impact they can have on you and how magical they really are. Many of my friends have had children over the past few years and I've been trusted enough to be a godparent to some, and even to change the odd nappy of others (my friends are so kind!). Babysitting duties often come around and I've become quite accomplished at telling bedtime stories – even if I do frequently fall asleep before the kids. But it wasn't until my niece Evie was born, in October 2006, that I really began to understand the huge delight that children bring into our lives.

Evie and her family live ten minutes away from my house, so it's always easy for me to see her and be a part of her life. From the moment I first laid eyes on her little face my heart melted, and even though she's only three we've become firm friends. She has her own sparkly pink 'princess' bedroom at my home for the nights she stays over, which happily have become more and more frequent. She has abandoned any attempt to call me 'Uncle', instead insisting on calling me 'Tone,' which sounds so cute coming from such a small child. She makes me laugh harder than anyone else I know and she's especially funny when she's telling me off for singing badly or mixing up the names of the characters in her books – God forbid I should get Peppa Pig confused with Upsy Daisy.

To hear Evie sing 'Twinkle twinkle little star' is a treat not to be missed; she doesn't realise it yet but I have recorded her so I can listen to her in the car when I'm away from home. Just this last December, we sang in the car together when I took her to a Christmas village all set up in a forest in deepest Kent. Along with Santa there were reindeer, huskies and actors dressed as elves – a look I personally wouldn't recommend, but they seemed to be enjoying themselves. Each child got to meet Father Christmas – the real one, of course – and Evie's eyes sparkled with anticipation as we awaited the allotted hour. Then one of Santa's little helpers came along and escorted us through the magical forest, adorned with thousands of fairy lights, to a wooden cabin hidden among the trees.

It was all so authentic that even I was getting excited. We were asked to take a seat on the porch and wait to be called. I will never forget the look of absolute wonder on Evie's face as she sat there wide-eyed, and then turned to me and whispered, 'We're going to meet Father Christmas, aren't we, Tone?'

Moments like these are so precious I wish I could bottle them; I now know at first hand that children are blessings, a gift from heaven to be cherished for all time. Discovering the powerful bond that can be forged between adults and children has not only been a complete joy but at times a much-needed reminder of what wonders there are to behold in this world. Only last week, Evie stopped dead in her tracks and stood open-mouthed for a few moments, staring up at the sky before exclaiming, 'How beautiful the stars are, Tone!' If she hadn't been with me I probably wouldn't have even noticed the stars were out.

While working in Spain with a friend not so long ago, we were introduced to an amazing woman called Maria, who had for many years worked with children. We spent the evening together at a local restaurant and she shared some of her extraordinary experiences with us. She told us that many of the children she worked with were from broken homes or had particularly challenging behaviour, and she sometimes felt she was running out of ideas, not only about how to deal with the kids on a day-to-day basis, but also how she might break through and help them create better opportunities for their futures.

When she shared her concerns with a friend one day, she was perplexed by the suggestion that she should try teaching the children to meditate. This was something she had never even tried herself and she couldn't see how it would be appropriate to a group of challenging and sometimes aggressive kids who wanted to be anywhere else but her classroom. After a particularly difficult series of episodes, however, she was about ready to try anything, and as a last ditch effort invited a meditation teacher to her class.

They initially started with six children, who were among the better behaved of the group, and Maria observed with great interest how the children remained attentive and still during the first guided meditation. This in itself was extraordinary as most of the time when she tried to get them to focus on a given exercise, she couldn't keep their attention for more than ten minutes. Yet here they were, eyes closed and seemingly relaxed and content for about half an hour.

After a few sessions, there was a remarkable difference in the kids' behaviour – not only while in meditation but, more importantly, afterwards, when they were far more amenable, polite and able to focus. Maris was so struck by these results that she tried similar meditation exercises with the most unruly and challenging children. These kids didn't display quite such favourable results, although the majority of them were able to sit still for at least ten minutes, and their behaviour for the rest of the day noticeably improved. After some difficulty in convincing her superiors, Maria gained permission to include meditation exercises in the children's schedule, between 9.15 and 10.00 a.m. every morning.

The meditations evolved very quickly. Each child was asked to visualise their favourite colour and watch it swirling in their minds, and then picture themselves wearing this colour and reflect on how it made them feel. This was just the start of many journeys that Maria had learned on how to guide herself, having great fun unleashing her creativity in the quest for different and stimulating 'places' to take the children. She would ask them to imagine that they each had a rucksack, which they would pack with their favourite goodies for the journey, they would then embark on a walk together, sometimes up on a mountain, sometimes along the shore by the ocean, seeing in their minds all the beauty and wildlife filling the surrounding landscape.

After a few weeks, the children started to suggest different things they might try for next time – 'Please, Miss, can it be the Amazon jungle?' or 'Somewhere with icebergs!' – and would then come up with their own very creative storylines for these adventures.

I listened to all of this with great interest, also feeling excited that this woman with a very traditional and formal background in teaching had the courage to think outside the box and be creative enough to try something different. I became even more fascinated when she described how, after just three or four weeks of daily sessions, the children really began to change. Beyond the fact that their concentration levels had improved enormously, even for the most rebellious kids, Maria noticed that they seemed to be acting in a kinder way towards one another, with more courteousness and a marked reduction in the level of bullying, which at one point had been rife among them.

A further, very positive development was that two of the girls in the class had seen each other in their meditations and felt strangely drawn to one another. They went on to form a strong friendship, which delighted Maria since until then both of them had found it difficult to create and sustain relationships within their peer group. Then, as a result of the new bond between them, they found it easier to reach out to the rest of the group and forge further friendships.

I was completely fascinated as I listened to Maria's story, but I had no idea that it was to become yet more intriguing. It transpired that the theme of the children's meditations had changed entirely when one of them asked if they could in the next session visualise a journey that was out of this world. Maria confessed that she'd been a little taken aback by this request and unsure how to respond. When she quizzed the child further as to what exactly she meant, she said, wouldn't it be fantastic to explore heaven? On this occasion, although she noted the girl's request, Maria did not feel comfortable pursuing it. She had no religious convictions of her own, or belief in the existence of a heavenly place, but more importantly she did not want to be seen to be pushing any kind of religious references down the kids' throats that might offend their parents.

But gradually more of the children asked Maria, either privately or within the meditation session, to take them to places that were beyond this world. They wanted to journey into the skies, see the stars, visit the moon – and perhaps even go beyond the universe and get a glimpse of heaven itself.

At this point Maria looked at me and asked if I'd ever seen heaven, and of course I told her that I had. She seemed reassured by this and went on to tell us that despite her reservations she'd been so impressed by the changes within the children that she hadn't wanted to curb their new-found enthusiasm. She therefore gently suggested to them that they should try to imagine what it might be like to look beyond this world, not necessarily to a place called heaven, but to a more perfect world, one that didn't suffer from the primary ills of our own.

From this moment on, even without any kind of religious references, many of the kids suddenly reported seeing angels or heavenly-type beings in their meditations. At first Maria thought it must be just their imaginations, reasoning that they would of course conjure up perfect beings in a perfect world, and so she didn't give it much more thought. As things progressed, however, even during very structured sessions where she would ask the kids to meditate on something specific like their school day or activities in the park, they still continued to give feedback about angels appearing. No matter what type of situation they envisioned, they would talk about the feeling of having a conversation with these angel beings or how their meditations would go off in a particular fashion that had no bearing on what the teacher was asking them to visualise. It was as though the kids were being guided on unique journeys of their own.

Although Maria didn't really give any sense of her own beliefs in relation to what the children were claiming to have seen, she was nonetheless incredibly enthusiastic about the progress they'd made as a result of these morning meditations. I was totally bowled over by what she told me, and when she asked if I would one day like to visit the school and see the children for myself, perhaps holding a meditation session with them, I promised I would do just that – and I'm greatly looking forward to meeting the kids once we've been able to arrange the visit.

Maria's story opened up so many fascinating questions on a number of different levels. Firstly, I wondered if the same kind of results might be achieved across the board – whether all children could potentially benefit from a regular period of quiet time, especially in these days of constant technological stimulation. If they were encouraged to calm their minds, focus and just be still in each other's company, I'm sure they would become far more receptive and therefore able to absorb so much more from the teaching that followed throughout the rest of their day.

I was almost overexcited by this possibility of inviting the other world close and allowing our young ones to be introduced and experience the love that emanates from these beautiful spirit people. How much more receptive would they then be to guidance from the other world? I believe that children should be individuals and I certainly wouldn't want to overstimulate their minds or push them in any given direction – they need to be free to find their own beliefs and views on the world, in essence to find their own truth. But I also believe that offering them the notion that there might be something beyond this world that is positive, joyous and healing might well give them the belief that they are loved by a greater force, and so allowing them to lead more well-adjusted and joyful lives. Even if they're just given food for thought – the option to explore and investigate in their own time and on their own terms the possibility of an existence beyond this physical world – then I for one feel sure that they would enjoy and perhaps benefit from the process.

From time to time, I'm asked to give a demonstration at social events that include dinner and drinks, and it seems the promise of a good meal and party atmosphere invariably attracts a very different type of audience from my usual sort of demonstration. At one such event, I'd just finished giving an after-dinner talk on the nature of mediumship and my belief in an afterlife, when a pleasant-looking woman in a spangly blue dress approached me. In a voice that hinted she had enjoyed the drinking part of the evening slightly too much, she introduced herself as Penny and then proceeded to tell me that her house was haunted.

'Uh-oh,' I thought as a familiar sinking feeling came over me. Usually when I hear something like this it tends to be inspired by an overactive imagination rather than the appearance of the spirit world – and it's difficult to point this out to the person concerned. This case seemed to be no exception and the more I tried to alleviate Penny's fears, the more animated and outspoken she became. We eventually reached the point where I thought the only way I was going to convince her would be to go to her home and see for myself what was going on.

Like a lamb to the slaughter I voiced this thought. No sooner had the words left my mouth than Penny had her diary out of her bag, ready to confirm a date and time for my visit. It just so happened that she lived in a town I was due to visit a few months later, so I arranged to see her before giving my demonstration there.

True to my word, on the day in question I found myself walking up the garden path of a well-presented 1970s detached house. On answering the door, Penny eagerly led me through to the lounge and immediately asked for my first impressions. I explained to her that I would need time to have a proper look round to get a real sense of her home and whether there was any spirit activity.

Other than the two of us, the house was empty. I left Penny in the lounge and wandered around the kitchen and dining room, even popping my head into the downstairs cloakroom. Much as I had expected, I picked up very little other than a nice, normal, family feeling.

As I climbed the stairs, I noticed the plush, creamy-beige carpet and felt relieved I'd taken my shoes off at the front door. I entered what I assumed was Penny's bedroom and then moved on to two further bedrooms of varying sizes. Each felt much the same as the downstairs rooms – all very pleasant and nothing to report. Somewhat out on a limb at the far end of the landing was another bedroom, which must have been built as an extension. As well as the separateness of this room, I was struck by the fact that the door was closed, whereas all the other doors in the house were wide open. A sign hung on it read, 'Ellie's room – keep out'. I smiled to myself as I opened the door, thinking, 'What the heck, she's at school, she won't know.'

I entered the room and my instant reaction was, 'Oh my God.' It felt completely different from every other room in the house. I stood for a while, absorbing the atmosphere and trying to identify what it was I was picking up. Visually, it was a very neat and tidy child's room, the walls freshly painted in pale lilac, the bed carefully made and no clutter lying around. Without any disrespect to Penny, this room was certainly the tidiest in the house. I sat carefully on the foot of Ellie's bed, taking care not to crease the immaculate bedspread, and closed my eyes in an attempt to clarify what was going on.

Remembering Penny's words, 'My house is haunted,' I opened my mind, sending a thought to both Zintar and Star, asking them to help me understand what was happening here. Quick as a flash, I felt the reassuring presence of both of them, standing on either side of me. Zintar spoke first, his words tumbling into my mind clearly and concisely. 'This is a special place,' he said. 'A meeting point between the two worlds, a place where heaven and Earth can easily merge.'

As Zintar's thoughts faded from my mind, Star spoke. 'Look to the corner of the room,' he told me. I looked and saw a small, white wicker chair adorned by a pink, floppy-eared toy rabbit – and nothing more. Knowing that Star would have had a reason for saying what he did, I continued to stare into the corner. After a few moments I saw a tiny pinprick of light, followed by another and then another. Presently there were a dozen or so, dancing like fireflies on a dark night.

As I gazed on, the lights grew in intensity, moving faster and faster, creating a continuous swirl of movement. And then, from deep within this phenomenon, there gradually emerged a face – one of the most beautiful I'd ever seen. It was also androgynous and from past experiences such as this I knew without doubt that I was looking at a truly advanced spirit being. Even though I'm used to seeing, feeling and sensing unusual things, it was still difficult to process what was happening. This was not something I was seeing in my mind, but a face so tangible it seemed that if I walked to the corner of the room I could have touched it.

This extraordinary spirit being then smiled to me and I noticed the most vividly blue, sparkling eyes. There was no need for words because I felt there was an innate knowingness connecting the two of us, and as I smiled back I seemed to be enveloped by an overwhelming feeling of love emanating from this being's beautiful soul.

All too soon, the face began to fade and once more the lights returned, one by one, only to disappear in turn, like candles beneath a snuffer. In a moment, I felt Star again, telling me, 'We are delighted that you have been able to see one of the others.' And I was delighted too – not only for having seen this being but for feeling the love that came from within.

At this point, I suddenly became aware of the most exquisite perfume. It was almost overpowering, as though hundreds of highly-scented roses had been left in the room. I looked around for any obvious signs of air fresheners, but there were none. And then I knew that this fragrance had been created by the spirit world and offered to me as a further indication of just how easy they found it to manifest in this room.

I have in the past smelled perfume from the other world, but never as intensely as now, in young Ellie's bedroom. I'm a great believer that the spirits find it easier to manifest or come close to us in places where there is a very positive ambience or energy – atmospheres that are filled with laughter and love and good intentions. I subsequently learned that the room was indeed a more recent addition to the house, having been used by Penny as a nursery, and so for several years it had been a happy, nurturing environment for babies and infants. Then Ellie, the youngest, had spent her whole life – ten years – there. The more I learned of the history of the family, the more I realised that there had only ever been love in this room. And so it made perfect sense to me that the spirit world would find it very easy to manifest in this special place.

Penny told me all this after I shared with her what I'd seen and felt. She seemed incredibly relieved that her home had been blessed with such a positive energy and that there was nothing to be worried about – her home was not 'haunted' in the way she had thought. When I asked her whether Ellie had ever seen anything in her bedroom, she replied, 'All the time. She's always talking about her imaginary friends – and not just them but my father too. He died before Ellie was born, but she often tells me of conversations she has with her granddad. I always thought she just had an overactive imagi-nation, but now I'm not so sure.'

I believe that places in our world where the spirit people find it easier to link with us should be respected and valued. You yourself might have encountered such a place, perhaps without appreciating it for what it was – a place where the energy has not been corrupted by negativity, trauma or sadness. So be aware that you might encounter such a place again, and if your spiritual awareness is more heightened than in the past you may be lucky enough to realise that you are standing between the two worlds – in a place where magic really can happen. Make the most of it and welcome your spirit people to you.

Children, whether they are alive in our world or dwelling in the other, are incredibly special. All they ask of us is to love them and allow them to grow and evolve to reach their full potential. But let us remember that we were once children too; it's never too late for us to rediscover the child within and live a more carefree and joyful life.

7
Healing with Angels

'If, instead of a gem, or even a flower, we should cast the gift of a loving thought into the heart of a friend, that would be giving as the angels give.'

George MacDonald

It is a simple fact of life that we all encounter difficulties on occasion, and I'm sure most of us can easily recall times that were filled with sadness, depression or despair, when we greatly needed the love and support of family and friends. Events such as the passing of a family member, the break-up of a relationship or hitting tough financial circumstances can be difficult enough to deal with, but sometimes life just seems to throw everything at us at once and it can feel as if our whole world is falling apart. It is at these times of great strife that many people look beyond the more familiar avenues of comfort and seek guidance from a higher source.

This is never more evident than when confronted by the life-threatening illness of a close family member or dear friend. The powerlessness we feel – the inability to change the course of events – is not only immensely frustrating but can also bring about deep sadness. When we truly love another, there is a part of us that would offer to take on their condition and suffer it for them if we could. To see the despair in a loved one's eyes as they look to us for reassurance and to know that we do not have the means to help them is one of the hardest things any of us has to face. When we've offered them emotional support, completed their weekly shop, run all manner of other errands and scanned the internet for rare and ground-breaking remedies – when there is nothing more to do than hope for the impossible, many turn to prayer. Even confirmed atheists or those without any great belief in an afterlife might find themselves being drawn to a church, mosque, synagogue or other hallowed place, or perhaps dropping to their knees in their front room, asking that God intercede to save those they love. Asking, in effect, for a miracle.

We all recognise that life in this world is finite. For the elderly, there is only a certain amount of time before the physical heart becomes too tired to beat. But in the case of a younger person, especially a child, serious illness can be much harder to bear. Nonetheless, we occasionally hear of an extraordinary turn of events in even the bleakest of situations. Of the many such stories I've come across over the last twenty years, one will remain with me forever.

At the end of a demonstration in the Republic of Ireland's wonderful capital city, Dublin, many members of the audience were kind enough to queue afterwards and ask me to sign books and brochures as keepsakes of the evening. I was speaking with the last few of them when my eyes were drawn to an enormous sequined butterfly on the T-shirt of a very attractive woman waiting to one side. I beckoned her over and asked if she'd enjoyed the evening. She said she'd had a wonderful time, but the reason she was waiting to speak to me was because she wanted to share an experience she and her family had a few months beforehand. Well, as with all these events, the theatre staff were understandably itching to lock up for the night and go home, so I suggested that this woman, who introduced herself as Alison, should tell me her story outside.

When we went out, there was a howling gale with rain lashing at us almost horizontally, so I suggested we should hop into one of the tour vans parked across the way. Fortunately, the rest of the crew had decided to travel together in the larger of the two vehicles we use and had given the keys to the other one to me. Moments later, Alison and I found ourselves sitting snugly in a Transit van while the foul weather continued outside.

Alison described to me her complete devastation when she heard the news that her only daughter Catherine had been diagnosed with a brain tumour, aged just twenty-nine. 'It was as if my whole world caved in,' she said. 'When I heard the words spoken out loud, I thought my very heart had stopped beating.'

The eventual prognosis for Catherine came as an even bigger blow when the family was told that she had no more than a few months to live. She was herself a mother, having just given birth to her second child, Emily-Jane, a gorgeous, bright-eyed, red-haired beauty, as her grandmother proudly described her.

For the first few weeks, Alison and her family walked around in a daze, unable to believe that such a terrible thing could happen to them. They were able, however, to draw a sliver of comfort from the fact that, for the moment, Catherine was relatively well in herself.

It was around this time, Alison told me, that Catherine saw me on television in an episode of 'Sixth Sense' with Colin Fry, who had kindly invited me onto his show as a guest medium. As Catherine watched me doing a reading for a member of the studio audience, a curious thing happened: out of nowhere, a red rose petal floated onto the floor of the room where she sat. There were no roses in her home at the time and she looked at the petal in astonishment, wondering whether her brain tumour was causing her to hallucinate. Only when she picked up the petal and held it in her hands did she realise that it was indeed very real. Gazing back at the television, she had an overwhelming feeling that this was a sign to seek me out; she had no idea why, but sensed that on some level I might be able to help her.

'That's where it all began,' Alison said. Unbeknown to me, mother and daughter had then followed my demonstrations from venue to venue, both in Ireland and the UK, not even sure themselves how I could help them; they were simply driven by the thought of the rose petal. I suppose when all hope seems lost, we try anything and travel anywhere in search of a miracle.

Although I was finding Alison's story deeply compelling, at this point I couldn't help glancing down at my watch and saw that it was five past midnight. It had been a very long day and I was desperately tired. But at that moment a memory popped into my head of a dear friend who had passed from cancer just months before, and that little thought made me wonder if perhaps the other world was trying to encourage me to refocus my mind and listen to this woman.

'You know, we've met before,' Alison told me. 'After your demonstration in Leamington Spa, Catherine and I asked you to sign a copy of one of your books. You took one look at us and said we must be mother and daughter as we looked so alike. But then you said something really weird.'

Apparently, out of the blue I told them, 'For some reason you're making me think of the mother and daughter, Miriam and Tirzah, in the film *Ben-Hur*. You don't look like them of course, but . . .' As I gave a little shrug, Alison and Catherine stood in disbelief as they had just watched the film together and it was one of Catherine's favourites. The mother and daughter in the story were struck down by an incurable disease and taken to see Jesus Christ in the desperate hope of a miracle cure. Alison told me briefly of Catherine's own plight and described how the two of them had empathised with the mother and daughter's struggle in the film.

'As they received their miracle and were healed,' said Alison, 'we were in floods of tears. I can't tell you how hard I prayed that night that the same could happen for Catherine.'

Apparently, on that night in Leamington Spa, our conversation was relatively brief, but as they were leaving I handed a single-stemmed red rose to Catherine. It had been given to me by another member of the audience, but I said to Catherine that as we were on tour for some days and the rose would no doubt be ruined, perhaps she would like to have it as a keepsake. All in all, both mother and daughter took this as some kind of a sign and the red rose and *Ben-Hur* reference seemed to reignite their search for a miracle.

Back in the Transit van with Alison, I found the story more fascinating by the second, though still battling against my tiredness. Recognising the lateness of the hour, Alison promised she wouldn't be too much longer but needed to tell me what happened next.

'A few weeks later,' she said, 'Catherine was absorbed in one of your books and reached the part about your experience in the pyramid.' Alison was referring to one of the Great Pyramids of Giza in Egypt, where a truly extraordinary thing had happened to me – I'd felt myself connecting with a great and divine force, and related in my book how this had completely changed my perception of life and the role we play within the universe. When she read this, an overwhelming compulsion came over Catherine and she told her mother excitedly, 'Come on, we're going to Egypt.'

Less than forty-eight hours later, the two women found themselves at the foot of the Great Pyramid. 'It was evening by the time we got there,' Alison told me. 'The sun was just setting and the sky was the most incredible shades of red and orange. We couldn't quite believe we were actually there, in this ancient place, looking at such a beautiful sight. And then this man approached us.'

Alison and Catherine were told by their tour guide that, for conservation reasons, it was no longer possible to enter the pyramids. So when a tall Egyptian man dressed in a long white galabeya suggested that if they wanted to enter they should follow him, they were understandably a little suspicious of his motives. Catherine, however, was adamant that she wanted to go in – this was why she'd come to Egypt and nothing was going to stop her. Alison was a little more circumspect, but wasn't about to allow Catherine to go on her own, so the pair of them followed the mysterious man deep into the heart of the pyramid.

'He spoke to me in broken English,' Alison said, 'but it was good enough that I could understand. He suggested I sit down and rest for a while and then looked at Catherine and held out his hand to her. While I wasn't sure of his motives when we were outside, I saw such kindness in his eyes now that I somehow knew I could trust him. He led my daughter to the middle of the central open area and suggested she sat down. Then he asked her to close her eyes.'

Alison paused here to tell me how she was brought up believing in God but was never quite sure about the spiritual side of things. What happened that day, however, changed her views forever.

'He asked if he could place his hands on Catherine's head,' she went on, 'explaining that he had helped people in this way before. Catherine asked him how he knew there was something wrong with her head, but he simply smiled and said, "Sometimes I just know." He seemed so kind and genuine that Catherine nodded for him to continue.'

Alison described how she looked on as the tall Egyptian gently moved his hands from Catherine's head to her neck and then back to her head again. Her daughter was totally comfortable and seemed more at peace than she had for weeks. Seeing this, Alison also relaxed and closed her eyes, soaking up the atmosphere and praying that some of the energy and power of this wonderful ancient place would help her daughter.

'I've no idea how long we sat there,' Alison said, 'but when I opened my eyes again, only Catherine and I remained. She looked different. I know it's strange, but I somehow knew that something had changed inside her. I asked her how she was and she said, "I feel amazing, on top of the world."'

Catherine related to her mother how she had seen an array of extraordinary colours in her mind, and that the Egyptian's hands had become so hot as he touched her that it felt as though electric currents were passing through her entire body.

When they made their way out of the pyramid, into the cool night air, Alison and Catherine once again encountered their mysterious new friend. 'You feel better now,' he said to Catherine. A little lost for words, she simply agreed that she did. He then escorted them back to the main street, where they tried to give him money for his time and trouble, but he would have none of it. He just smiled and wished them God's blessings. And then he turned and disappeared into the crowd.

'We came home a few days later,' Alison continued, 'and Catherine went for a prearranged hospital scan. The doctors were baffled by the results: Catherine's tumour had gone. It had disappeared completely and they had no idea how it could have happened. But, of course, we knew.'

I was naturally enthralled to hear this true tale of healing, one that defied all logic or scientific explanation. I thanked Alison for sharing it with me, and as she opened the door of the van to leave, I asked her, 'Who do you think the man was?'

She gazed back at me and then gave a gentle smile. 'He must have been an angel,' she said.

It's a heart-warming and uplifting story, but sadly not everyone is so fortunate. I remember a spiritualist medium I used to work with called Marcia Ford, who told me how she would visit her mother-in-law almost every day and give her spiritual healing, calling on those in the other world to assist in her endeavours. You might think that someone who was receiving this amount of energy on a daily basis would be fighting fit and full of vitality, and yet the old lady still seemed to encounter the same coughs, colds and ailments as anyone else. And then one day, she got up as usual in the morning and by the afternoon she had passed.

So swift and unexpected was her passing that an autopsy was requested. The results revealed that she had been suffering from an advanced form of cancer, affecting her stomach, bowel and liver, which she must have had for a considerable time. She had not, however, suffered any pain or other symptoms that might have indicated she was so ill. I believe in this case the healing had nonetheless worked – and worked beautifully. I can understand that many might question this, believing that all healing should result in an absolute cure, but sometimes it works in mysterious ways. Marcia's mother-in-law not only passed at a good age but had led a full and active life until the end, maintaining her dignity and being spared the chronic effects of her dreadful illness. Marcia agreed that her own prayers had truly been answered and that working with the power of love and assistance of her spirit guides had bestowed on her mother-in-law a true blessing, one that had allowed her to remain well for the duration of her physical life.

I think this particular story is fascinating because it helps us to look at things from a different perspective. This life we live is our present reality and so the thought of losing those we love, even if we believe we will see them again, can seem terrifying. Learning to see things in a different way must surely assist us in coming to terms with circumstances that might otherwise be too hard to bear.

I have already mentioned earlier in this book how I believe that illness comes to us as a consequence of our being housed in a physical body that sometimes malfunctions – it's not something dealt out by a puppet master in the sky. Recognising this is liberating, as we can then focus on ways of maintaining good health by generating positive energy to balance our mind, body and spirit, thereby embracing the knowledge that we can work closely with our guides and angelic friends in the other world to bring the blessings of healing to those who seek it from us.

Spiritual healers had something of a heyday during the time of the two World Wars, when the demand for healing was at its height. As you might imagine, not only were people physically damaged by acts of war, but for many the emotional turmoil was too much to bear. Never before was there such an immense need for some form of physical, mental or spiritual assistance.

The majority of healers came from a spiritualist background. After years of training and learning how to work with their individual guides, they worked selflessly, offering healing sessions to anybody who asked them. Many of these sessions were carried out after the public meetings of local spiritualist churches. Following the divine service or an evening of mediumship, chairs would be quickly rearranged and the healers would take up their positions, spending around ten to fifteen minutes with each of the many 'patients' waiting in the queue.

Such healing practices are still very much in evidence in our modern-day spiritualist churches and centres. This is a testament to the popularity of the spiritualist philosophy and it gives me a warm feeling to see this reminder that spiritual healing is alive and well after all these years.

There are many people sorely in need of healing and the work of our guides and angelic friends who never have the opportunity, or perhaps desire, to enter a place where this might happen. Fortunately, the spirit people in their wisdom work with diverse people across the world, entering into the minds and philosophies of countless individuals, so that we now see hands-on healing carried out in orthodox religious gatherings, at New Age festivals and even in your local beautician's on the high street.

Whether such practices are referred to as angelic healing, reiki or other names, in essence they are one and the same. The process for the healer begins when they recognise deep within themselves that they have something to offer and that they are guided and helped by an unseen force. They know this force to be one of love and they want others to feel it for themselves. There are thousands of people like this throughout the world, with many and varied titles such as shaman, wise elder or New Age therapist. The way they practise and the name they are given is determined by their culture and location, but essentially each of them recognises that they are loved by a powerful unseen force, and as part of their own soul's progression they wish to find a way of tapping into and focusing that energy to impart goodness into the world. They do this for the benefit of the individual through the process of healing, or for the many by helping to create positive and loving environments for all to enter. There are now more opportunities and greater freedom of expression in this arena than ever before.

Talking of freedom of expression, I once heard while working in Denmark of a local 'healer' who would insist on taking off all his clothes during a treatment session because he felt his nakedness allowed him to be far more open to channelling good healing vibrations. This is not something I will be doing any time soon, you'll be pleased to hear. I was also told of someone who would perform healing by placing his client at one end of a very long hallway as he charged at them from the other end, shouting and screaming in an attempt to banish all negativity. I wouldn't want to disparage any particular healing method, but to me it goes without saying that far greater benefit is derived in a nurturing, spiritual and professional environment where potential clients feel at ease. In my experience, the more relaxed a person feels, the more they stand to gain from the healing experience.

I've no doubt that, given the number of people we encounter on a day-to-day basis who are experiencing pain on various levels, many of you reading this book will want to play an active part in this healing revolution. This may not be as difficult as you might think. A tremendous amount can be accomplished by learning how to work with thought and good intention – the power of our minds is a phenomenon that never ceases to astound me. So, the next time you encounter someone you know is in physical pain, you might like to take a moment to look on them with absolute kindness and a love that feels as if you are embracing your nearest and dearest. Now visualise them surrounded by a vibrant white light, and then hold them in this light each time you think about them from that moment on. This simple process of sending positive energy from you to them, with the strong intent of wanting to make them feel better, may have a profoundly beneficial effect. It's an incredibly straightforward exercise, representing only the first stage in an apprenticeship that could ultimately see those who are pure in heart performing deeds that might be perceived as miracles.

If you prefer something slightly more tangible to set you on the path towards spiritual healing, you might want to consider the following practical steps to help you on your way.

I would suggest you purchase a notebook from your local newsagents – your own 'healing book' – and jot down the names of anyone you can think of who might be in need of healing at this time. You may choose to write by their name why you believe healing is necessary, for example, back pain, illness or grief; it's not that the spirit people need to know but it might help to remind you of this person's need to receive.

Then, each night before you go to bed, sit with your book in your hand, close your eyes and speak to the other world. It's not necessary to do this out loud – which might come as a relief to your other half – simply send the spirit people your thoughts, perhaps along the lines, 'Dear friends in the other world, family, guides and angels, please help me in sending healing to all those whose names appear in my healing book. I ask this of you in love and I pray that you will assist with God's love.' Then visualise each person's face in turn as they appear in your notebook, seeing them bathed in pure white light and recognising this light as the source of divine love.

When you have considered everyone in your book, you might wish to thank the spirit world for their assistance.

I know we are all different and while the above techniques might be sufficient for some of you to begin to see wonderful results from your efforts, others may prefer a more gradual approach, in which case more detailed steps follow, as well as a sample meditation, towards the end of this chapter.

Traditionally, miracles have been seen as phenomena from a bygone age, occurring thousands of years ago and far outside anything we might expect to see in our own lifetimes. But in truth, from the creation of life to the moment of death, miracles are happening all the time. My first real taste of this was something that took place when I was about nineteen and still working in an office in London.

It was freezing cold as I hopped from foot to foot at the bus stop one morning, trying to recover some feeling in my toes. Never at my brightest at 7 am, I'd forgotten to bring a hat or scarf and so pulled my jacket collar high to shield my ears from the biting wind. As I did, I became aware that an elderly man next to me was watching my efforts to combat the extremes of the weather. He wore a battered trilby at a jaunty angle over his thin grey hair and his slightly loose clothing suggested he had once been a much bigger man. When I looked into his watery blue eyes, he struck me as a rather defeated and lonely character, which was borne out by the tone of his voice as he muttered, 'I'm glad I don't have to do this every day.'

I responded by telling him that it was very much a part of my daily routine, catching the bus to catch the train and then the Tube that would get me to my office for 9 am. We struck up a conversation, and in the ten minutes or so before the bus came, he managed to squeeze in a potted history of his life story. His name was George and his wife had left him some years before, then his only daughter had emigrated to New Zealand, leaving him all alone. He was very open and forthcoming in telling me how he found it hard to mix and make new friends, which seemed all the more tragic when he confided that he'd even lost his beloved dog recently, his constant companion for the last fifteen years.

I listened intently as we continued to chat on the bus. Then we reached his stop and I waved him on his way. I thought little more of this encounter for the next few weeks, but then as if by chance I started bumping into George almost everywhere I went – in the post office, the doctor's waiting room or the checkout queue at the local supermarket. It sometimes felt as though he appeared from nowhere, but we chatted each time and a bond began to form between us.

At around this time I was participating in a small mediumship development group run by my old tutor, Joan Barham. One evening, Joan looked at me and said she had a strong sense that the spirit world had sent me a rather lonely, elderly man who they hoped I would be able to assist. I could only think of George and wondered what on earth the spirits wanted me to do for him. Joan suggested I should send him some healing, although I must confess that at the time I wasn't entirely sure what that even meant, let alone how to do it.

'Picture him in your mind,' said Joan. 'Visualise him clearly, then bathe him in pure light and ask the spirits to assist you.'

So that's exactly what I did. From that day on, both morning and night, I sat for a few minutes picturing George enveloped in the purest white light that I could conjure, and asked in my mind that he be assisted. This in itself is no easy feat. Trying to stop my mind jumping from one muddled thought to another, through the events of the day to what I needed to buy for supper and what time I might get the dogs' last walk in, tends to make it rather difficult to focus on the job in hand. But, practise makes perfect, as they say, so I persevered.

Some months passed and George was nowhere to be seen. Then one day I suddenly saw him on the high street, walking towards me with a young woman on his arm. I must confess to feeling totally astonished. I knew it was George but he looked as though he'd been given a Trinny and Susannah makeover. From his clothes and hair to his new trilby hat, he looked fantastic: he'd put on a healthy amount of weight, his eyes were sparkling and he seemed at least ten years younger.

My surprise must have been self-evident since George shook my hand reassuringly and said, 'I know. Weird, isn't it? I feel like a million dollars. It's as though someone's switched a light on after all these years.'

He then introduced me to the young woman, who turned out to be his daughter. They had fallen out some years before, but not so long ago George plucked up the courage to call and try to resolve their differences. His attempts at reconciliation had gone so well that he then jumped on a plane to visit her in Auckland, where he had the time of his life. His daughter subsequently decided to take a holiday herself and visit her dad, and so here they were, strolling down the high street.

George was to all intents and purposes a changed man. I remember discussing this with Joan and telling her I wasn't sure whether any of this metamorphosis might have been down to me. 'Very little to do with you, young man,' Joan explained to me kindly. 'And everything to do with the spirit world.'

I know Joan was right, but it still came as a revelation that I might have played even a tiny part in something so wondrous. I will never forget the experience because it showed me just how effective positive thought can be, especially when created in a loving way and accompanied by a genuine desire to help another human being. Even though the positive change was instigated by the spirit world, and George had been open enough to be receptive to their work, the fact that they had heard my prayers in the first place, and taken on board my intentions, made me feel very humbled.

It was suggested to me by other members of Joan's circle that I might like to try the practice of contact healing. They explained that the same positive thoughts could be employed while placing my hands lightly on an individual in need and that the results could be far more powerful. So one Sunday evening, as the meeting of a Spiritualist Church ended, I was invited to work alongside the healers of the Church. This being my first week, I was asked to work with a young woman called Pauline. 'Watch me,' she said, 'and then I'll ask you to join in part way through.'

Our first client bustled in, a regular at this kind of meeting. She looked resplendent in her ornate purple hat and reminded me a little of the Queen Mother. Our charge looked me up and down suspiciously, no doubt aware that I was young enough to be her grandson. Then she sat down, closing her eyes and placing her hands on her lap, palms open, in the customary way.

'She's done this before,' I thought to myself, 'she knows what to expect.' I said a silent prayer of thanks for Pauline's presence and the fact that I was not being unleashed on this woman on my own.

Pauline positioned herself behind the woman, placing her hands gently on her shoulders and then closing her eyes. I watched, enthralled, as her breathing became deeper and she seemed to enter a trance-like state. By now I'd seen this kind of phenomenon a number of times, but to see it so closely, at first-hand, caused a rush of excitement through my entire body. I was mesmerised by the controlled way Pauline's hands moved around the woman, from the top of her head, down to her ears, to her shoulders, down her back, and then finally as she ran her hands along the woman's arms the healing appeared to be complete. 'All done,' I heard Pauline say as her elderly charge opened her eyes.

'That felt wonderful,' she responded with a deep sigh. As I heard these words, I was struck by how truly wonderful it was. Observing in this way had been a real eye-opener for me; although I was used to seeing the spirit world in action through the messages they relayed via the medium each Sunday evening in church, this was different. I also realised just how involved the spirit people were within the healing discipline.

'Right, your turn,' Pauline suddenly said, jolting me out of my reverie.

I was extremely nervous, not wanting to let down either the recipient or the spirit people. I took my place and waited for the next patient to enter. My heart sank a little when I saw a young woman clutching two crutches and being helped into the room. I knew her through the church; her name was Andrea, and she suffered from some type of rare hereditary disorder. Doctors had told her parents she was unlikely to live beyond the age of thirty.

'Oh for pity's sake,' I thought, 'what do they expect of me?'

Andrea was a lovely woman, always smiling and with kind words for everyone, but I was at a loss as to what I could possibly do for someone with a condition as serious as hers – not least because this was my first ever attempt at hands-on spiritual healing.

I guess Pauline picked up on my grave doubts because she placed her hand reassuringly on the small of my back and gently nudged me forward. 'Just place your hands on her shoulders,' she instructed me quietly. 'Then close your eyes and I'll talk you through what you need to do.'

I did as she said, then she told me to call on my guide and asked whether I knew his name. 'At least I can do this bit,' I thought, before asking in my mind, 'Zintar, where are you? Please help me.' And then, quite extraordinarily in the circumstances, I became aware of Zintar's presence at my left-hand side. My heart began to thump and I still felt out of my depth, but Pauline's voice was reassuring. 'Ask your guide to place his hands over yours,' she said. 'Remember, it's not you giving the healing, it's the power of the spirit world working through you.'

After a few moments, I realised that my hands had started to shake slightly and felt warmer than they had before. At first I questioned this, wondering whether it was simply down to my nerves and the heat created between my hands and the soft angora jumper Andrea was wearing. This thought had barely entered my conscious mind when I felt my hands rising up towards her head. But these hands were no longer my own; they had been surrendered to Zintar and it was he who was manipulating them from Andrea's ears, to the top of her head, the front of her face, the nape of her neck, on they moved. They felt hotter than ever before and remained a little shaky throughout the episode.

And then, as though someone had pulled the plug from the mains, it suddenly stopped. Knowing that the healing session was over, I opened my eyes and asked Andrea how she felt. I was a little disappointed when she didn't leap from her chair and run around the room, declaring, 'Eureka, I'm cured! It's a miracle!' Instead, she said she was fine and then got to her feet very slowly, supported by her crutches. She thanked me kindly and made her way out of the healing room.

I turned to Pauline and said excitedly, 'That was amazing. I've never felt anything like it. I can't believe how powerful it felt.'

Pauline smiled and told me I'd done very well, but advised, 'Next week when you heal, don't be surprised if it feels a lot less intense. The other world may have laid on a special show for your first time, just to demonstrate to you how powerful healing can be.'

And she was right. Week after week, I healed with Pauline, each time hoping to re-experience the extraordinary vibrations I'd felt that first week, yet never really achieving the same sense of intensity.

Andrea still came to me and the other church healers every week and I worked with her occasionally over the next six months. What happened evolved slowly. After some months, Andrea was able to walk with only one crutch. There was never anything dramatic like, 'Stand up, throw away your crutch and walk,' but I had no doubt that the work of the spirits was having an effect. Andrea's whole persona had changed and her attitude brightened normously, bringing about a vast improvement in her condition. After our last healing session together, she took me to one side and said, 'I'll pray for you now, that you may always be blessed by the spirit people. You can't know what you've all done for me.'

A few years ago our paths met again. Andrea still walks with a stick and nowadays seems a little more frail than when I last saw her, even though she is a relatively young woman. But she remains unruffled by this. 'I have defied the doctors,' she told me. 'They wrote me off years ago, but I'm still here, by the power of spirit.'

I was so pleased to see her again after all these years, and our meeting reinforced to me that although healing might be deemed successful in benefitting the recipient and blessing their lives accordingly, it will not always result in a complete cure.

I was once asked what exactly healing energy is and it took me a while to vocalise my thoughts. My explanation was something along the lines that the loving force, or energy of the Great Spirit, surrounds us at all times and has the power to make us feel better on many levels. This power is there for the taking; it can be received at will when an individual opens their mind and heart to invoke it, directing it to places in the body or mind to bring about physical wellbeing and clarity of thought. Learning how to do this successfully takes time and perseverance. And bearing in mind that most people who wish to receive healing need it immediately, it makes sense to suggest they seek out an experienced spiritual healer

As I say, the ability is there for the taking and not a gift bestowed only on the spiritual elite. Anyone with a caring heart, a genuine sensitivity and a desire to serve and benefit others is an ideal candidate. Invariably when I meet this kind of person, there is an obvious gentleness and selflessness to their demeanour – they are quiet, calm individuals who often think of others before themselves and recognise that the spirit people not only exist but also want to help us in this field. For those of you who wish to pursue the method of healing further, the suggestions below might help.

But first, because we will be looking at the process of meditation, if this is new to you allow me give you a little guidance on one of the most important parts of the process, namely your breathing. It is vital that you begin a meditation by focusing all your attention on your breathing since this helps calm the mind and makes it far less likely that you will allow random problems or worries into your thoughts.

I generally inhale to the count of ten and then exhale, also to the count of ten. I breathe through my nose the whole time, but it doesn't matter if you prefer to breathe through your mouth. If you find it a little difficult at first, count to a lower number and try to build up gradually. The idea is that you learn to control each inhalation and exhalation, and by focusing on and practising this process you will still your mind very quickly – and in so doing will hold the key to all future spiritual work.

Let us now look at the gradual steps that will assist you on your journey towards working with the spirit world to facilitate healing.

1. For the first seven days, set aside twenty minutes of your day to sit in silent contemplation, clarifying anything you might need to address in your life and being thankful for all the positive things that surround you. This is a time to evaluate who you are, celebrate your triumphs and identify any obstacles that might hamper your further development.

2. For the next seven days, take twenty minutes out for a gentle meditation. Try sitting in the meditation position – with your eyes closed, hands relaxed and your back straight and comfortably supported. Focus on your breathing, as we've discussed, so that you become calm and centred. Now try to visualise yourself healthy and happy and dressed in pure white clothes. Imagine your unseen friends from the other world gathering close to you, trying to make your acquaintance.

3. In the third week, I would suggest working towards blending with your unseen friends in the other world. One of your friends in the other world will try to merge his or her energy with yours and they will be more successful in this if your mind stays focussed on each incoming and outgoing breath.

4. By the fourth week, it would be wonderful if you had learned how to still your mind and surrender sufficiently to the loving influence of the other world so that you were ready to take the next step – that is, make a connection to the healing force that surrounds all living things. Once you have merged with your guide, consider the world around you, the natural world in which we live, and focus on bringing positive, healing energy into the atmosphere, for the benefit of all life in our world. If you would like to try sending healing to specific individuals, I suggest you look at the meditation I have set out below.

5. By week five, your friends in the other world will have become familiar with you and recognised your efforts to reach out to them and their world. So open up and allow yourself to be influenced by their guidance – learn to 'listen' to the inner voice that brings knowledge and understanding.

For those of you who feel able to follow these points successfully – and remember they are only guidelines for the new enquirer – we can go a step farther. I am a strong believer in the power of invocation – that is, requesting from a spiritual force the power of loving energy for the benefit of others. Before trying the meditation below, I would suggest you read through it a few times, so that you become familiar with the feel of the journey. Be aware that it might have a profound effect on you, for if you complete it successfully you may go to a place of enlightenment and thereafter be open to the power and inspiration of the angelic realm.

MEDITATION

Before you start to focus on your breathing, get yourself in the right frame of mind by reminding yourself that you are a beautiful spiritual being with the potential to forge an incredibly powerful connection with your spirit guardians and angels in the other world. They await your invitation to gather close to you so that you may begin a strong and long-lasting relationship with them, in the knowledge that this powerful bond will help facilitate inspiration and healing in our world.

Believe that you are loved. No matter who you are or where you dwell in this world, you are loved by the creative force of the universe and the angelic beings who guide you. Just know this and free yourself to love in return.

Now, relax your body and centre your thoughts so you can begin to embrace the spiritual aspect of your being, ready to look beyond yourself and become conscious of the healing power of the universe – a pure white light, an immensely positive energy that has the ability to heal and transform and is naturally attracted to you as it emanates from the powerful, loving source that surrounds us.

Focus on your breathing, keeping it as slow and steady as you are comfortably able, and then imagine that the pure white healing light is filling your nose and mouth and moving on to circulate throughout your entire body. Now see this light emanating from you and flowing around the room where you sit.

Bring all your awareness to your forehead and to your heart, as it is here that we may sense the other world clearly.

Using the creative, imaginative faculties of your mind,

now see yourself standing by the edge of a beautiful lake. Visualise its safe, calm waters, the shimmering light of every colour that dances gently across the surface as the sun caresses each gentle ripple and motion.

Imagine yourself standing ankle-deep in the shallow water at the edge of the lake and feel the coolness of the healing water as it laps softly against your bare skin. Look down at your body and see that you are dressed in a white robe, beneath which your body is strong and healthy. Picture yourself gazing across the lake, the waters that seem to stretch out to infinity, and become aware of a silver, ethereal mist that swirls before you.

Watch as the mist begins to thicken, and as it does, within its centre a beautiful angelic being appears before you. Gaze at your angel, becoming aware of their appearance, seeing the colours that emanate from them and taking time to allow them to observe you too.

As you look at the face of your angel, repeat in your mind: 'Angel friend, guide me into light. Angel friend, journey with me into light.' Now become aware of your angel friend opening their arms and holding you; allow their energy to course through you as they draw you upwards and into their embrace. Surrender all rational thought and open up your mind to inspiration; they will wish to commune and give guidance, as well as offer healing to you and your chosen loved ones.

When you wish to return to every day consciousness, simply imagine yourself back into the room where you sit, remembering to send up a thought of thanks to your new spirit companions.

To begin with, you may find that your spiritual journey lasts only a few moments. But with determination and the desire to forge a stronger connection with those that dwell in the higher realms of the spirits, these experiences may last for half an hour or so. You will no doubt experience something different each time you take this meditation, discovering new horizons as your spiritual evolvement continues.

I wish you well on your journey of giving. Through your thoughts and through your actions, may loving energy flow from you and little miracles be achieved.

8

A Journey Quest

'Angels can fly because they take themselves lightly.'

Anon

Every now and then we all need some down time, a quiet place to lay our heads, somewhere to switch off from the crazy whirl of our everyday lives. I've been lucky enough to visit many countries around the world, often for work but also on holiday. Without a doubt, one of my favourite places is the Spanish island of Gran Canaria.

Situated off the coast of Morocco, Gran Canaria is the third largest of seven major islands in the Canarian archipelago. One of the main attractions for me is the diversity of the scenery – the central volcanic mountains, fertile valleys, pine forests, banana plantations with steeped terraced slopes, the vast sand dunes at Maspalomas and even the low-lying arid landscapes to the south-east of the island. All this, coupled with year-round sunshine – Gran Canaria has been described as the 'land of everlasting spring' – makes it hard to beat. Little wonder, then, that it provided the setting not so long ago for one of the most extraordinary days of my life.

I first went to the island on holiday about fifteen years ago for some rest and relaxation with a group of friends. The main intention at the time was to commandeer a sun lounger and lie on it for an entire fortnight, with a tall glass of cool, local beer close to hand. On the way home, I vividly remember feeling a tremendous sense of loss as I waited at Las Palmas airport: the island and its people had really got under my skin and I was very sad to leave.

Needless to say, within a few months I found myself returning to Gran Canaria, and this time I had to accept that I was hooked. I've continued to visit a few times a year ever since, and I have to say that swimming in the clear, azure-blue ocean, beneath the most fabulous cloudless sky makes me feel totally alive and at one with my surroundings. For the first couple of years I thought this sense of peace was simply the result of such a pleasant climate, but I have since come to recognise that something more takes place when I'm there – a special energy emanates from this place that completely resonates with me.

I'm not suggesting that everyone who chooses to visit the island will feel exactly the same way as I do – we are all unique and your special place of resonance might be anywhere between Kenya, Canada or Cornwall. But suffice to say, no matter how tired I feel from the constant cycle of travelling around giving demonstrations and lectures, the moment I step off the aeroplane and stand on the island's soil, I'm met with the overwhelming sense that I am home.

So strong is the pull of Gran Canaria that I will at some point consider living there full-time, but at the moment this would be impractical since I need to be based in a place that allows me to travel easily around the UK, as well as being close to an international airport. A few years ago, however, I came up with a cunning plan that would give me the best of both worlds, and I now have a modest, yet lovely bungalow in Gran Canaria, nestled on a hillside overlooking an area called Maspalomas. I consider myself truly blessed that I can fly off occasionally and allow myself time to recuperate in my beautiful little house on the hill.

Before I bought the house, I must have looked at dozens of potential properties, but the moment I set eyes on this place I knew it was right for me. As I walked through the front door, I saw a kitchen that looked like it should be condemned, a bathroom that reminded me of something out of the TV show 'DIY SOS', and built-in cupboards that had reached the firewood stage. Trying to see beyond the huge amount of work that needed to be done, I asked myself why I would want this place over any of the others I'd seen. The answer was that it just felt right. After years of telling other people to go with their hunches when something feels like it's meant to be, what else could I do but buy it?

The renovations are now complete and this little home has become my sanctuary, my tiny piece of paradise – so much so that I've named it 'Cielo', which in Spanish means 'heaven'.

When I was there a year or so ago, I woke up unusually early one morning, the sky ablaze with orange as the sun began to appear. Normally I would have closed my eyes again and fallen back into sleep, but I felt strangely awake and full of energy on this day. So I jumped out of bed and straight into the shower. With my hair still wet, I pulled on some shorts and ventured out into the garden, sitting myself down in my favourite space – a tiny corner surrounded by vibrant purple and white bougainvillea. I sat for a while, mesmerised by the colours and heavy fragrance of the flowers all around me, feeling totally at peace.

Then into this tranquil space came a reassuring presence and I heard in my mind the voice of my guide, Zintar. 'The day is beautiful,' he observed. 'May we share it with you?' I was only too happy to give my permission.

I sat there a few moments, wondering whether Zintar would continue to speak with me, but no further words came. Instead, I received a strong clairvoyant image of a place I had so far only seen in travel guides for the island. I knew this was the Roque Nublo, a spine of hard volcanic rock that sits atop the second-highest peak on the island, and is thought to have been the core of a volcano formed about three and a half million years ago.

The vision was incredibly powerful and I had a strong sense of déjà vu. I hadn't been to this place before but somehow felt that I knew it, and knew it intimately. Without understanding why, but believing that the spirit people were drawing me there, I felt an overwhelming need to travel high into the mountains to see the Roque Nublo for myself. I couldn't help smiling because I realised that my uncharacteristically early and zestful start to the day was all part of a higher plan, orchestrated by my spirit friends. So how could I ignore their request to share this day with me?

As I got ready for my excursion, I felt like a small child going to a friend's birthday party – I wondered who would be there and what excitements lay in store for me. I packed a few provisions in my rucksack – bottled water, bananas, two boiled eggs and a Curly Wurly – and also stuffed in a fleece as I had no idea how cool it might be up on the mountain. Without further ado, I jumped into my hired white Renault Clio and was off, with Krishna Das music playing all around me.

Before long, I left the main dual carriageway and started to wend my way along the narrow, bendy roads that led up towards the mountains. After driving for a little while, I came across a small viewpoint at a place called Degollada De Las Yeguas and parked the car. A handful of people were taking photographs from the viewing platform's edge and I walked out to join them. Even from this comparatively low height, the view was spectacular, the majestic rocks rising out of the vast, arid and unforgiving landscape reminding me of an old

Western movie. The terrain was scarred by a criss-crossing of dirt tracks and I couldn't imagine who would travel along them or where they might lead.

I stood there for some time, waiting for some sort of profound revelation, or at least the presence of the spirit people, and couldn't help feeling disappointed when nothing came. Then I suddenly felt compelled to look up to the sky, and there, soaring high above me, was an enormous bird that looked like an eagle. As if recognising that I'd spotted it, it swooped down in front of me and into the valley below. I was surprised that nobody else noticed this huge bird of prey, but perhaps they were too absorbed in taking photographs and chatting among themselves.

As I was about to move on with my journey, I closed my eyes, just to see if I could feel the presence of the other world. And there he was – Zintar. I could see his face in profile and felt encouraged that he was still with me. I'm not sure how much longer I drove on, but when you're concentrating with all your might on narrow roads with hairpin bends and a sheer drop beside you, all I can say is that time passes very slowly. There was no shortage of road signs for the Roque Nublo so I felt reassured that I was heading in the right direction.

The nearer I got to my destination the stranger I began to feel. As hard as I concentrated on the road and signs, it felt as though someone was trying to lead me in a totally differ- ent direction. The whole thing felt like a mental tug-of-war between my rational mind clearly saying, 'The mountain is incredibly steep and dangerous. For goodness' sake stay on the road,' and a stronger force urging me to take another direction entirely. So, perhaps foolishly – but as I'm sure you're aware by now, not entirely surprisingly – I did.

Still winding around the mountainside, I encouraged my reluctant Clio along a hazardous dirt track for a little while, all road signs now having disappeared. I knew I couldn't be far from the Roque Nublo and yet had no idea where I actually was.

Rounding yet another tight bend, I was suddenly confronted by a large billy goat gazing lazily back at me from where he sat in the middle of the road. There was no room for me to pass, so I tried a polite toot on the horn. Despite the fact that we were in the middle of nowhere and there can't have been many vehicles passing through this area, the goat looked as though he'd seen it all before and was completely unperturbed. I leant out of the window and, feeling I should at least do him the courtesy of addressing him in his native language, tried a quick 'Vamos!'

No deal, not even when I added for good measure, 'Er, por favor?' It was a stand-off. The goat was going nowhere and therefore neither was I. It was impossible to turn the car around, and as I mulled over what to do next the thought came to me that perhaps I just needed to wait and have a little faith. I looked about me and realised I could reverse a few feet into a small gap between the rocks at the roadside. As I did, I remember thinking to myself, 'OK, this is where you've been led.' And my next thought was, 'So what the hell do I do now?'

I got out of the car, smiled cautiously at the goat as I passed him and carried on up the track on foot. As the terrain was quite rough, I wished I'd worn sturdier footwear than my not-so-trusty trainers, which scuffed uncomfortably against the dry and stony ground. I plodded on, the sound of my footsteps the only thing I could hear, until I became aware of another noise behind me, which also sounded like a set of footsteps. At first I thought it might be some kind of echo created by the rocky landscape or altitude, but as I continued to walk I realised that the rhythm of the steps was completely different from my own. Suddenly alarmed, I spun round, fully expecting to see some moustachioed bandit in a striped poncho about to launch himself at me – but there was no one. Not a soul in sight.

I'm not easily spooked but this was a little too close for comfort. I may receive visions, hear spirit voices and pass on messages from departed loved ones, but when it comes to being followed up a remote mountain track by someone or something I can't see, I begin to wobble a bit. My heart racing, I cautiously checked whether someone might be lurking behind the cluster of rocks at the side of the path, but again there was nothing there. And then as I glanced down at the path I'd already trodden, I saw I wasn't imagining things – there were indeed two sets of footprints, side by side in the dusty earth. As I examined the second set more closely, I was astonished to see they'd been created not by shoes but bare feet. I double-checked that they hadn't continued on ahead of me, and realised that this phenomenon must have been the work of the spirit people – I'd been joined by someone from the other world who wanted to make their presence felt in a physical way. Even the most experienced mediums, with a steadfast belief in the afterlife, are not beyond requesting physical evidence from time to time. So to think such evidence had been presented to me in this way – and unsolicited at that – was really exhilarating.

As I stood dumbfounded, I suddenly heard Zintar's voice – and I don't think I'd ever been so pleased to hear from him. 'He belongs to this place,' he told me. 'Allow him to lead you from this point onwards.'

Finally reassured that I was in safe hands and that Zintar was still watching over me, I closed my eyes and became aware of my unseen friend. I sensed he wanted to introduce himself and allow me to know who he was, and that the easiest way of achieving this would be to allow our minds to blend together. I sent out a thought to him, 'Come close to me, friend.' Then I began to focus on my breathing, taking slow, steady breaths, trying to calm my conscious mind. Within moments I began to feel his presence within me.

I knew this was the spirit of an ancient tribal person, born of this land many hundreds of years before. His bare-chested form was muscular and athletic, his hair much longer than my own and he held a cane in his right hand. All these impressions flooded into my mind in an instant, and with them came the desire to open my eyes and allow him to look through them. A wave of emotion ran through me as we shared together the view of the fabulous landscape stretching out before us.

After a few minutes I felt the intensity of the spiritual connection subside somewhat, but now that we'd been introduced I was confident the tribesman would remain with me and show me the way as I continued my journey towards the Roque.

Feeling consumed and exhilarated by the experience, I seemed to be making much faster progress than before, finding myself off the dirt track and scrambling over rocky terrain as we climbed higher and higher. Suddenly there it was – the Roque Nublo itself, standing tall and proud, pointing up towards the heavens. I had made it.

As I gazed on this majestic sight, I began to understand why I'd been guided away from the well-worn tourist tracks to view the Roque from a completely different standpoint. The fact that I was in a place where very few people would ever have stood meant that the innate energy of the land had not been distorted, and I saw not only the rock in all its natural beauty, but felt the powerful energies emanating from it. I'm not one for idolising objects or monuments, but there was something truly spectacular about this place – its atmosphere was so powerful I felt sure that here prayers could be heard and blessings granted.

As these revelations entered my mind I realised they were coming from my tribesman companion, who was by my side sharing the experience with me. There have been few moments in my life when I've felt so completely at ease with myself and my surroundings, and I had an overwhelming sense that I was truly in the presence of the Great Spirit.

I sat for some time, feeling deeply contented and open to the inspiration of the spirit world. And then the tribesman began to reveal to me details of his former life and why he continued to devote himself to this ancient, mountain-top place. As his thoughts blended with mine, he showed me with great clarity how he and his people considered the rock to be a sacred place and possessed of supernatural powers. At certain times of the year, according to lunar and tidal cycles, every community on the island would travel here to make offerings of food and gifts to the gods and give praise to them in exhibitions of dance, chanting and singing. Unlike in certain other tribal communities, where religious teachings were undertaken exclusively by men, women were highly valued and their equal status meant they could attain the most senior ranks in the tribe. Even the religious leader of this very spiritual community would be chosen not by gender but by the purity and wisdom they exuded.

All this information came to me with such ease and detail that I felt I was aware of every part of these ancient memories of my tribesman companion. And then, clairvoyantly, I saw very clearly men, women and children building and lighting enormous bonfires. I became completely engrossed as I watched them dancing and singing, their faces illuminated in the darkness by the powerful orange glow from the fires. It all felt so incredibly real to me that I could not only see the activities but also absorb the joy and mutual respect among those celebrating being together that night with fire, food and music.

But suddenly, these impressions stopped. I remained in my receptive state and patiently waited for fresh imagery to flood my mind, but there was only silence and darkness. I stared into the inky blackness in my mind for what seemed like a very long time and then I noticed it begin to swirl. It's difficult to describe exactly, but the darkness seemed to develop a movement and texture all its own. I found myself a little perplexed by this phenomenon that felt like a vision, yet with nothing to see. But then I began to understand what was happening; while the vision itself continued, I was now wearing a hood over my head – thick and black, with no openings for the eyes. Feeling jolted by this bizarre realisation, I mentally lifted the hood from my face, only to find that I was sitting in a circle of people, all with the same hoods pulled down over their heads. I counted nine of us in total, each sitting on the ground in complete silence. Sending a thought to the tribesman, I asked him, 'What is this? What are you showing me?'

The answer came back directly. 'This is how the sensitive ones among our people received guidance from the gods. They believed that by sitting within the group, denying themselves sight and sound, they would receive more powerful messages and guidance for their people.'

He went on to impress on me how his people's ethos for life was based on sharing and harmonising with their natural environment. Great emphasis was also placed on building strong relationships with one another, mutual care and support between every member of the community being considered as important as giving praise and thanks to the spirits above.

Learning of these simple philosophies had a profound effect on me, for there was great humility and love underlying this uncomplicated way of living. I can honestly say that I felt blessed to have witnessed a small slice of that life and now try to carry its principles with me as I go about my day – making a little more effort to live every moment for its own sake and investing more time and care in my own family and friends and in everybody who connects with me. With the stresses and strains of modern-day life it's not always easy, but I do at least try. I wonder how much our society might benefit if we all held the view that everyone who comes into our day, whether sharing a meeting room, a carriage on the Tube or an aisle in the supermarket, is a part of the same spiritual community and should be given the same respect and consideration our forefathers gave to those around them.

On that day at the Roque Nublo, I had been so engrossed in and amazed by the level of detail my tribesman companion had imparted that, when a sense of déjà vu again swept through me, I wanted to ask him whether we were in some way spiritually connected. But before the question could properly formulate in my mind, the answer came.

'Yes, we are connected. All will become clear one day.'

It is a day I'm still eagerly awaiting, and I suspect is another lesson in patience for me, though I have no doubt all will be revealed in the fullness of time.

In any event, it seems the tribesman assumed no further explanation was necessary at that time because I immediately felt his link with me begin to dissipate. I became far more conscious of myself, sitting alone, gazing towards the Roque Nublo, which I was now looking at with a totally new insight. The place I had initially thought of simply as one of great natural beauty was now imbued with profound spiritual significance – somewhere I felt I had visited before, long ago, and knew one day I would return to. It was a place that had truly touched my heart.

Eventually, I stumbled to my feet and slowly began my descent towards my car. When I arrived, I was surprised to find the billy goat still lying in exactly the same spot; perhaps he really was a guardian to this gateway to a most magical place. I like to think that he paid me so little attention because he'd been tipped off in advance about my visit, although he showed no sign of recognition of my profound experiences there. He gave me a sidelong look as I bade him 'Adios, amigo' and got back into the now swelteringly hot Clio.

I had to get down the mountain somehow and since I now knew the track ahead petered out as far as the passage of a vehicle was concerned, there was no alternative but to attempt the impossible. The length of my relatively small car, set against the very narrow dirt track, was a ratio I did not particularly wish to contemplate and, grateful though I was to my tribesman friend, I had no desire to join him in the next world just yet. So I set about my task with extreme caution and, despite some decidedly wobbly clutch control at times, managed to inch back and forth through a twenty-eight-point turn until I successfully manoeuvred the car so it was facing back down the track.

I spent the next hour or so marvelling at the fantastic scenery as I descended the mountain, not really sure which direction to take but not much caring either – I just knew that wherever I ended up was where I was meant to be. There were a number of small signposts on this labyrinth of mountain roads and I recognised from one that I was near one of several mountain lakes that peppered the landscape. A few minutes later, I found myself looking not at the pond I had anticipated, but the most enormous expanse of water, a truly breathtaking sight. I jumped out of the car and made my way to the edge of the lake where I crouched down, running my hands through water as clear as crystal and still cool despite the heat of the day. I splashed my face and the sensation was so refreshing that there was only one thing I wanted to do next. But there was also one big problem: no swimming trunks.

I can assure you I'm not in the habit of taking my clothes off in public places, but there was not a soul to be seen and I'm afraid my desire to cool down overwhelmed any potential fear of embarrassment. So I stripped off down to my underwear and stepped up to my ankles in the water. But before I went any further, I was struck by another urge. Maybe it was because I'd just turned forty and life in this world is short, but after another furtive look around I whipped off my remaining garment and took the plunge.

I was still half expecting a busload of tourists to turn up and had visions of having to remain in the water until they'd gone; or, worse, the Spanish policia might make an appearance and I'd do my next bit of sightseeing from the inside of an armoured vehicle. I decided I didn't care. Here I was, swimming au naturel in a glorious mountain lake on Gran Canaria, feeling fabulous at forty and completely liberated.

I floated lazily for a while, stretching out and unwinding, listening to the birdsong along the shore – I'm sure they started chirruping more heartily as the last of my clothes came off. I gazed at the tall trees on the banks of the lake and, turning onto my back, at the vast, cloudless blue canopy above. I felt amazing. I've always found it so wonderful to be aware of the spirit world and so enriching to know that each of us will journey on to something more than this physical life, but to appreciate this while surrounded by such earthly beauty seemed to intensify and magnify the reality. After a while, I found myself feeling quite emotional – not through worry, stress or concern, but elation. I spread my arms wide and floated on my back, as happy as I had ever felt in my entire life.

I don't know how much time passed, but eventually I swam nearer to the shore and lay down on the pebble floor below the shallow, warm water, letting it lap gently against my body. I remained there a while longer, marvelling at the experiences of my day, and as the water lapped over me it felt as though I were being cleansed, healed. An immense sense of physical and mental wellbeing came over me and by the time I got dressed and returned to my car, I felt wonderful – completely alive and a good ten years younger.

A glance at my watch told me it was now 3.50 pm and as I didn't really know where I was I thought it would be a good idea to head for home. Trundling up the road, catching a last glimpse of the lake in my rear-view mirror, the thought of returning to my little house on the hill felt most enticing, and after a few wrong turns and dead ends, I eventually found myself back on the right road.

As I had existed on snacks all day, my thoughts inevitably turned to what I was going to eat for my evening meal. In my mind I conjured a sumptuous feast, but in reality I knew there were only tomatoes and mozzarella in the fridge. I was just planning what I would need to buy to have with them when I felt Zintar come close. Sadly, I had to put all thoughts of food to one side because he impressed on me the strong sense that the day was not yet over – the spirit world had another experience in store for me.

While following the signs for Maspalomas, I came to a village called San Bartolome and was immediately struck by its appealing, whitewashed buildings set in narrow streets festooned with flags and balloons in readiness for a forthcoming festival. I pulled over to buy more water for the rest of the journey and, confident I wasn't too far from home, I decided to have a little meander around. A few people were still going about their business yet there was a lovely air of peace in this tiny place, enhanced by beautiful, light-operatic music drifting from an open window above a grocer's shop.

Presently, I found myself standing outside a large church called San Bartolome de Tirajana. I hovered a moment, uncertain whether or not I would be welcome to enter. I peeped in and was surprised to see a splendid, opulent interior. Rows of highly polished pews stretched out in front of me and all was silent within. As nobody else seemed to be around, I decided to go in. I wandered around for a while, taking in the fabulous architecture and statues and then I stood in the main aisle, trying to imagine all the thousands of people who had prayed here over many hundreds of years.

When I heard someone entering the church behind me, I looked around to see a middle-aged woman, casually dressed in a long, dark skirt and white blouse. It seemed as though she had the weight of the world on her shoulders, and not wishing to intrude on her visit I moved out of the aisle and sat in a nearby pew. As the woman was about to pass, she stopped and spoke to me in Spanish. Since my knowledge of the language pretty much extended to ordering a cup of coffee and telling a goat to move on, I replied somewhat feebly that I didn't understand. With a heavy sadness in her eyes, she nodded and slowly walked on, right up to the altar, where she stopped, made the sign of the cross and then sank to her knees to pray.

It wasn't any of my business, but the fact that this woman had chosen to pray where she did, rather than taking a pew as was more customary, made me think she must be in urgent need. I couldn't help wondering about her circumstances and why she might be feeling so desperate, but because of the language barrier I felt powerless to assist.

Then suddenly, from the corner of my eye I caught a movement to my left and assumed someone else had joined us. But when I looked across, there was nobody there. No sooner had my gaze returned to the praying woman than once more in my peripheral vision I saw movement. This time, I realised that what I was seeing was not a person at all but a kind of energy – nothing tangible, but something that resembled a heat haze. As it moved towards the woman at the altar it intensified, gradually beginning to take form, slowly at first then far more rapidly, until I could clearly see the figure of a young man. He seemed to be in his early twenties and was short, slightly built with black, close-cropped hair and wearing blue jeans and a T-shirt.

As the young man looked down at the kneeling woman, I knew instinctively that he was her son. As soon as I made that mental connection, he turned and looked directly at me, as if he knew I could see him. His expression seemed to convey a hope that I would tell his mother that he was there, but of course he had no idea that I couldn't communicate with her even so far as daily pleasantries, let alone impart a message about her deceased son and the afterlife. Feeling helpless, I shook my head slightly and gave him an apologetic smile.

The young man seemed to understand and turned to refocus his attention on his mother. I watched enthralled as he knelt down, wrapping his arms around her and I somehow felt that although she couldn't see him she would feel his presence and his touch. At that moment she began to utter long, keening moans, as though releasing her grief from the core of her being.

I then heard the woman speaking softly, and although I didn't understand what she was saying, I recognised the words for 'love' and 'heaven'. Both she and her son remained in their embrace for some minutes before the young man kissed his mother tenderly on the cheek and moved away. Then, when she rose to her feet and turned, she seemed barely recognisable as the woman I had seen before. She was smiling elatedly and as I watched her leave I noticed how she stood much taller now and walked with a purpose – everything about her was so much lighter and brighter. I couldn't know whether she'd been as aware of her son's presence as I had, but clearly something had happened to bring about such a positive, healing transformation.

By the time I looked back towards the altar, the woman's son had disappeared – but when I closed my eyes I could see him clairvoyantly. He too had a smile on his face, and without the need for words, whether Spanish or English, he bade me farewell.

I felt so touched to have been present at this exceptional and moving scene, and it made me realise that such an experience with the spirit world is possible for everyone. The participation of a medium is not always necessary for a powerful connection to be made: where true love exists, the bond can never be broken. Understanding why Zintar had wanted me to witness this reunion between mother and son made me feel incredibly humbled. As a medium I'm often the intermediary that allows bereaved families to be reunited, via messages from their loved ones in spirit; but here, I played no part in that process. I nevertheless felt immensely privileged to have been an observer to such a wondrous event and sent up my thanks to my spirit friends for guiding me to this place.

Feeling drained but happy, I made my way back to Maspalomas without further adventure, other than a quick trip to the supermarket to buy a few things to go with my tomatoes and mozzarella for supper. As I sat on the terrace that evening with a glass of cool, white Rioja, I reflected on my day, one that even for me had been filled with more spiritual adventures than any other, before or since. It had been a day very much orchestrated by the spirit world and I will look back on it for many years to come as truly out of this world. I have yet to journey back to the mountains of Gran Canaria but look forward to going again soon – and will be ready and prepared to experience all that those in the other world wish to share with me.

9
Bringing Spirit Into Your Life

'It is better to conquer yourself than to win a thousand battles. Then the victory is yours. It cannot be taken away from you, not by angels or by demons, heaven or hell.'

Buddha

It was a Thursday night and the weather outside was so foul that any sensible person would have stayed at home with a good book or tuned in to their favourite TV programme. But I pulled on my waterproof coat, tugging at the hood to protect myself as best I could against the bitter cold and teeming rain, and left the house at full speed. I was about eighteen years old and in those days I could run pretty fast, so what would have been a fifteen-minute walk was completed in record time.

I arrived out of breath at Harry's 1930s, semi-detached house. He answered the door, as always impeccably dressed and with his ever-present smile. He must have been well into his seventies by then and was rather frail and painfully thin, though no one ever heard him complain.

As he ushered me into his back room, I saw that I was the last to arrive. Assembled before me were the remaining members of the development circle, a small, dedicated group of people who sat weekly to develop their psychic gifts. Joan was the teaching medium and the half-dozen of us in her charge were raring to go and eager to learn from her.

On the dot of 7.30 Joan announced, 'Come along, it's time.' Carafes of water and glasses were collected from the kitchen, and one by one we climbed the steep, creaky stairs to the circle room, which was Harry's spare bedroom. On entering, we each took our own seat, designated to us when we first joined the circle. Joan leaned forward and lit the candle positioned on the table in front of us. The room fell deathly quiet as she opened the evening with a solemn prayer, asking our guardians and a host of angels to gather close and meet with us in this sacred space. I loved it when she called it a sacred space because it was such a simple room in a very ordinary house, yet it felt completely special. My heart would always beat a little faster as I took my place within the group, because I was never quite sure what would happen.

As I listened to Joan, I was struck by the sincerity and devotion she exuded, and then I felt a heightened sense of anticipation as she brought her prayer to a close with a soft, 'Dear friends, we leave this evening in your care.'

No sooner had these words left Joan's mouth than there was a tangible difference in the atmosphere. It's hard to describe how silence can be noisy, but now it was almost deafening and I knew something was about to happen. As I continued to look towards Joan, I noticed she had entered into a deep trance – her breathing became slower, her eyes were tightly shut and her face seemed almost featureless in the subdued light.

I was obviously still quite inexperienced and nearly jumped out of my seat when a booming, masculine voice filled the room. I looked at Joan and realised it was coming from her. The rest of the group, far more au fait with this kind of communication, greeted our spirit visitor warmly, along the lines, 'Welcome friend. Thank you for speaking with us this evening.' And there was I, transfixed, not quite believing I was really here and hugely excited about what might happen next.

The voice speaking through Joan was that of a spirit guide. The other members of the circle chatted away to him in a very casual manner, and once these pleasantries were over he turned his attention towards the most junior member of the group: me.

'Young man,' said the guide, 'we are pleased to see you here, so youthful and yet so willing. This evening we bring you a special visitor.'

Well, if I was excited before, I was beside myself now – who on earth would want to come to speak to me?

'I have a lady here,' continued the guide. 'She comes to you from our world and wishes you to know that she loves you very much.'

'Wow,' I thought, 'it's going to be my nan.' At this time in my life, she was the only person I had truly loved who had passed over and I wondered what it was she wanted to share with me.

'This lady stands now behind you,' the voice boomed again, and I have to confess I took a sneaky peek, but as there was nobody physically there I duly focused my attention back on the guide.

'She places a necklace around your neck and upon this is the Star of David.'

'Well, he's up the creek with that one,' I thought. My nan certainly had a necklace and my mum had that necklace after she died, but there was no Star of David on it, only the figure of Capricorn, Nan's birth sign.

Reluctant to interrupt while I was being spoken to, I allowed the guide to continue. Then I sat up in surprise and confusion when he announced that this woman was from Germany, spoke both English and German and had followed the Jewish faith during her lifetime.

'Do you know who she is?' the guide asked forcefully.

I was convinced the guide had it wrong, but I was after all a guest in this place and didn't want to be rude, so I took a deep breath, plucked up my courage and said, 'I'm sorry, but I've no idea who this lady is. My nan came from Walthamstow and she certainly didn't speak German – though she knew a few choice words in English.'

Unperturbed, the guide continued, 'Well this lady in spirit is connected with you and loves you. She is one from our world who has taken an interest in you. She watches over you and one day will prove this to you.'

The guide then thanked us for our time and attention and bade us farewell. After a few moments, Joan regained every-day consciousness and asked if we were all satisfied with what we had heard. We were all delighted that the spirit people had come through for us and told her so. Then she looked directly at me, enquiring, 'And what did the guide tell you, Tony?' I explained to her as succinctly as I could that I had received a message from a woman I didn't recognise. She smiled gently and advised, 'Be patient. Sometimes the spirit people bring us information that at first makes no sense, but it's usually clarified at a later date.'

How right she was, though it was a good eighteen years after this event that Joan's words rang true, when a chance meeting in North Wales confirmed to me just how amazing the spirit people can be.

Shortly after I'd finished giving a demonstration, a middle-aged woman approached, pushing her mother in a wheelchair. The mother spoke first: 'Hello, love, I'm your great auntie.'

Once in a while, people come up to me and make slightly strange claims, and now here I was, looking at a woman I'd never met in my life but who professed to be a relative. I stared at her for a moment with my mouth open, and the only word that came out of it was 'Oh.'

If she'd had any sense she'd have left it at that, rather than claiming this vacant-looking imbecile for her nearest and dearest, but she continued undeterred.

'My brother was your grandfather. I'm your Auntie Irene.'

'So . . . what was your brother's name?' I asked, trying to appear on the ball.

'Arthur.'

Well, Arthur was indeed my dad's father's name, but I'd never met him. Having abandoned his wife and children when my dad was eight years old and my uncle ten, my grandmother was left to bring up her two sons single-handed.

From her purse, Irene handed me several old black and white photographs. 'That's me and your nan,' she said.

As I gazed down, there was the face of my grandmother at the age of around seventeen, and I knew without doubt that I was indeed related to this woman. It's a little bizarre to meet somebody in this way, discovering that you come from the same ancestors and share the same blood when you have never previously heard of them; you are to all intents and purposes strangers.

We spoke for a while and Irene expressed her interest in the spirit world, making me wonder whether this trait ran in the family. But before I had a chance to ask her, she started telling me about her grandmother, my great-great-grand-mother, who had travelled from Germany as a young Jewish woman some time before the Second World War and settled in England to make a new life for herself. As I listened to the story unfold, my mind suddenly jumped back to Joan's circle meetings all those years before and how the guide had told me, 'One day she will prove this to you.' Now, at last, she had been true to her word.

Irene looked at me and said, 'I don't know why I'm going on about her, I haven't thought about her in years. I wanted to talk to you about your granddad.'

I smiled to myself, knowing that Irene had been inspired by the spirit world to tell me the story of this young woman who had waited all these years to confirm her presence. Since then I've felt her come close to me on numerous occasions and it's comforting to know who she is and why she's there.

Not long after meeting Irene I was asked to give a demonstration in aid of a Jewish organisation that supported victims of violence. I was introduced afterwards to an elderly woman by the name of Rose, who explained that she was also a medium and had worked quietly from her own home for many years. While we were talking, I became aware that she was looking over my shoulder, so much so that I looked round a couple of times thinking that somebody else had joined us. Then all of a sudden, Rose seized my hands and asked if she could describe someone she could see standing behind me.

'There's a lady in the other world,' she said, 'who's taken great interest in you and your work. She places the Star of David around your neck and tells me that she is your great-great-grandmother and loves you very much.'

Just as I was marvelling over the fact that this lady was here again, a strange thing happened. Rose told me that many of my ancestors had perished in the Holocaust. Despite my surprise, I listened quietly, struck by Rose's conviction. She was adamant that this was so, even though I didn't know I had any Jewish ancestry. I told her I had no idea about any of this but she said I should just be patient – given time, the spirit world would confirm the details. So I'm waiting, with absolute certainty that one day Rose will be proved right, just as Joan's guide had been almost twenty years earlier.

Thinking back to Joan's circle, I'm reminded of another question that arose some two decades ago, the answer to which has only recently been provided by the spirit world. This one relates to the very room I've described to you at Harry's house where Joan's circle sat. Hanging on the walls were framed portraits of various spirit guides from across the ages and around the globe, one of which, directly behind my seat, depicted a Native American Indian. His face was young and handsome, his hair as black as night and he wore a traditional headdress adorned with a single feather. I remarked one day how beautiful this portrait was and Joan told me it had been painted by the psychic artist Rosa Parvin, who was known for creating the most exquisite likenesses of the guides, guardians and angels of those who went to her for readings.

At a later meeting, Joan once again caught me gazing at the painting and said, 'You really like this picture don't you, Tony?' I said I thought it was wonderful; it was as though the young Indian's eyes saw straight inside me and I felt there was some kind of special connection between us. Joan smiled and said, 'I feel it too. I don't know why, but there is something about this picture that ties the two of you together.'

Not long ago I gave a charity demonstration for my old spiritualist church on Canvey Island – the church where all this began for me, where I first met Joan and went on to develop as a medium. Afterwards, the church president, Mavis, handed me a gift, wrapped neatly in pink crepe paper, as a thank you for the help I'd given them with some fundraising. I opened the present and my jaw dropped in amazement – there in my hands was the stunning portrait of the young Indian guide.

I told Mavis that I knew the picture but hadn't seen it in twenty years. She explained that it had been donated to the church a few years previously and she'd felt inspired to present it to me. I thanked her profusely and for days afterwards couldn't get over how this picture had come back to me all these years later. For me it illustrates the wonderful plans the spirit world has in helping us understand that they really do guide us and that there are moments of complete synchronicity in our lives where mysteries from long ago might be unravelled.

I'm aware that the gift I've been blessed with is not only about me – as a medium given survivalist evidence from the spirit world – but is about so much more. I continually receive evidence almost of a grand plan, a certain order of things, and how miraculous events can occur that defy logic or coincidence. These are for me a clear indication of just how close those in the spirit world are to all of us.

Of all the incredible experiences I've had, some of the most profound and powerful have occurred when I've invited the spirits to me while in a place created and set aside for this purpose. To begin with, it was the small back bedroom in Harry's home, and then Room 7 at the College of Psychic Studies where I often did one-to-one readings, as well as the large lounge at the Arthur Findlay College for spiritual advancement, and now my own modest teaching studio in Wickford, Essex.

I believe these places, set aside exclusively for mediumship and psychic work, have over a period of time become saturated by goodwill and positive endeavour, and consequently the spirit world can make their presence felt far more easily in this type of environment, rather than, say, someone's front room that has never been used for this purpose. Whether the furnishings are plush or modest makes little difference to the atmosphere of the room, which is created by both living and spirit people, those with an earnest desire to meet halfway between this world and the next.

It is far easier than you might think to create a space like this in your own home. You could allocate a spare room for the purpose, if you're lucky enough to have one, or if your home is overrun with children and all the paraphernalia of family life, there might be a part of your bedroom that could be designated as a 'hallowed place'. If you are genuinely interested in finding a greater connection with the spirit people and angel beings, you simply need to find a space you can retreat to, where you can sit peacefully and learn to blend with the minds of those who guide and guard you – and where the angels might have the opportunity to inspire you.

Once you've chosen your special space, I would suggest you clean it thoroughly from top to bottom, and while vacuuming and polishing try to imagine you are cleaning away all negativity, such as any residue of rows, hostility or feelings of depression. Simple thoughts like 'I wish to cleanse, heal and rectify all that has gone on before here' can have a powerful and lasting effect on the atmosphere. Go to the four corners of the room, clapping your hands enthusiastically in each; the noise and movement this creates, coupled with the power of your own cleansing thoughts, will help break up any stagnant energy.

The spirit people find it much easier to enter our atmosphere when it's positive and happy, so why not throw caution and self-consciousness to the wind and sing out loud – who cares whether the neighbours can hear you! It doesn't matter that you don't have the voice of Katherine Jenkins or Aled Jones – the spirit world will not be giving you marks for your performance – it's more important that you sing with gusto and enthusiasm, doing your utmost to create a tremendous positivity in this space.

By carrying out these simple actions you are beginning to create a special sanctuary all your own. But be patient – this is just Stage One. I would suggest that you try to spend time within this environment every day, but if that isn't possible then as often as your life allows. Sit in quiet contemplation, demanding nothing from the spirit people – at this point you are simply getting used to sitting in silence and training the mind to focus and receive impressions. Equally important, you are adding something of yourself to the atmosphere.

Once you feel comfortable with this, you might choose to learn the following affirmation: 'Great Spirit, allow me to know you as you know me. Angelic beings, allow me to see you as you see me. Dear spirit guardians, allow me to love you as you love me. Friends in the other world, gather close to me.'

Repeat this in your mind five or six times and when you are a little more confident hopefully you will feel empowered to speak it out loud. The most important part of this process is how you repeat the affirmation. When it is said or thought with absolute conviction, with love and a true desire to build a connection and a friendship with those who inspire us from the other world, it is my sincere hope that they will respond. For some people, the response comes tangibly and very quickly, but we are all different, so if you find you are not aware of any response, don't be disheartened – rest assured the spirit people are still there working with you and trying to facilitate a connection, which I hope will come to you in time.

After a period of practice with the affirmation, I would suggest that you incorporate a visualisation while you repeat it. When you ask that you might know the Great Spirit, imagine you are looking out at the most incredible sunset you've ever seen. Create a vibrant palette of colour – deep oranges, vivid purples, startling reds – and allow these colours to blend with you and touch the very centre of your being. When you ask that you may see the angels as they see you, visualise beings of light standing all around you. See their arms outstretched towards you and see your own arms outstretched in readiness to receive them. When you ask that you may love your guardians as they love you, imagine a host of spirit beings, men and women of all races, gathering close to you. See each of their faces in turn and feel their unconditional love for you. When you consider your own spirit family, allow there to be no sadness, but visualise them around you, smiling, happy, free of pain and contented in their new spirit life.

I hope that this combined affirmation and visualisation will act as a catalyst for future spiritual explorations – and of course you can also try the meditation techniques we touched on in Chapter 7. But remember, to be truly successful you have to want it wholeheartedly. Those who try the process with fear or disbelief will find themselves gazing about their newly-created sanctuary with thoughts only of tomorrow's shopping list, the school run or other everyday concerns that have no place in your special space.

I should say, of course, that not everyone is born to be a medium, but I genuinely believe that everyone's life can be touched and enriched by spirits and angels. So persevere and above all have patience – all good things come to those who wait.

From my own point of view, because I travel from venue to venue and country to country more than ever these days, it has become increasingly difficult to sit in a designated and attuned space. I have therefore become used to creating the right environment pretty much anywhere and often with only a moment's notice. So a modest hotel room can be transformed in seconds, simply by lighting a candle and switching on my music. I usually perch myself on the end of the bed – feet firmly on the ground, hands resting lightly in my lap, palms up – and then close my eyes, place all my concentration on my breathing and send up a thought for the other world to join me.

No matter where I travel throughout the world, my iPod goes with me and on it there are a thousand wonderful tunes that help to centre me in a matter of moments. Even at a busy airport, sitting on a train or more commonly waiting in the wings of a theatre stage before going on to give a demonstration, I can readily enter a space of serenity where I feel the spirits gather close.

Over the years my choice of music has changed dramatically. When I first began I listened to gentle, soothing music in an attempt to calm my mind, but now I've mastered this I go for something quite different. I mentioned Krishna Das earlier and I first stumbled on his music a few years ago when I purchased a CD of his called 'Pilgrim Heart'. The hairs on the back of my neck stood on end when I listened to track 2, entitled 'Govinda Hare', and I became quite emotional as I allowed this beautiful music to wash over me. Part way through the track I felt Zintar standing to the side of me. I was aware of his love and compassion for me, but also that he was bringing another person from the spirit world to me. No sooner had I realised this than there was an almost instantaneous blending of my soul with a being I somehow knew to be angelic. I couldn't distinguish its gender, but the overwhelming feeling was very feminine, soft and gentle.

The music continued to play and Krishna Das continued to sing, yet I felt transported into a different reality. The whole experience lasted as long as the song itself, no more than four or five minutes, but those moments were intense, precious and very different from other episodes. It wasn't as though I'd been whisked off to another place or journeyed to the spirit world; I was still aware of sitting in the room and listening to the music, but I felt this angel being and I were as one, that my thoughts were her thoughts and I was completely understood by her. I felt the form of her spirit body over my own and the robes she wore touching my body. I sensed her desire to impart spiritual truths to me, so I endeavoured to surrender my mind completely to her, and I believe now it was this willingness to receive her thoughts that allowed it to become possible.

In an instant my mind was awash with the most glorious inspired thoughts. She shared with me the wondrous philosophy that we are indeed all the same, that our lives are intrinsically entwined, that each of us has the capability to reach angelic status in time and that she herself had walked our world many years before. Through kindness, giving and sharing she had attained a state of enlightenment that allowed her to progress to the angelic status she now enjoyed. Her parting thoughts to me were very powerful: 'Allow others to know that they too have ultimate potential and are able to set themselves free from the shackles of material life and begin their journey towards finding happiness and truth while in this world.'

My angelic visitor moved away, leaving me with the lasting insight that we can all walk with angels and live a life connected to them. The song faded and the brief silence between the tracks brought me back to a more conscious state of mind, though I knew Zintar remained by my side. I continued to sit in a meditative state for some time, listening to the music and just enjoying being with Zintar. There was no need for words or other revelations to be received; it was like spending time with your very best friend in the world, listening to a concert or watching a play, and we simply sat together, happy to be in each other's company.

It was an unforgettable experience, and since that time I often choose to listen to the same kind of music as it seems to take me to a place where the spirit people connect with me very easily. I appreciate that this particular musical effect may be unique to me, but I would suggest you try to find music that resonates with you in a special way. There are thousands of titles to choose from, so enjoy the process of discovery. You never know, it could lead to something you might struggle to find with meditation alone – the right type of music for you could be the key to your own very special, profound connection with your angels and spirit friends.

As you've probably gathered by now, people often come up and chat to me after my demonstrations. On one such occasion I spoke with a very honest and open woman who said that although she believed in the spirit world, she really struggled when it came to believing in angels. She had no difficulty with the concept that her mother and father were in the spirit world and able to communicate with her, either directly or through a medium, but she couldn't believe in angels because to her they were all about God and she didn't believe in Him. So as far as she was concerned, there was an afterlife, but it was one with no God and no angels.

Over time I've been surprised to find that this is a commonly held belief. Now and again I ask people about their thoughts on the subject and it seems a number of them have similar ideas to this woman. I must confess that I find it slightly confusing that they could believe in something which many people find difficult, namely the spirit world, but not the rest of the 'equation' – that is, God and the angels. I guess it all comes down to life experiences. It seems that many people brought up with a traditional religious background but have chosen to turn away from it – perhaps feeling disillusioned, dissatisfied or unfulfilled – have then received evidence of an afterlife. Yet despite the fact they have seen that there is life after death, they find it difficult to make the connection between an everlasting life and the existence of the God force and our angel friends.

It's not for me to preach to these people and push my thoughts and philosophies on them, but when I get involved in these discussions I obviously discuss my own beliefs. I sometimes feel it may be easier if we try not to see God in a traditional religious way, but rather as a loving force, or energy, of which we are all a part – a force that is creative, beautiful and forgiving. Every one of us is guided, loved and helped by all those who have gone before us and who now dwell in the spirit world, each at a different stage of evolution. The truly evolved – those many would regard as angels – hope to inspire and instruct us so that we might live more generous and fulfilled lives.

For those who believe in these advanced spirit beings, the next question is often, 'So how can we become more open to them? How can we assist in bringing through information and guidance?'

I would suggest starting each day with a clear thought in your mind along the lines, 'If I may be of service this day, allow me to serve. May inspiration flow through me – I am willing to participate with my angelic friends.' These simple thoughts will act as an invocation, giving permission for those in the other world to gather close to you and begin a process whereby you eventually become far more aware of their presence and able to act as they direct you.

When I say this, I mean for you to live your normal day, going about your business as usual – collecting your kids, mowing the lawn, preparing supper and all the tasks we tackle on a day-to-day basis. But we can do all these things with an awareness that the other world wishes to inspire us. The way they do this is by guiding us in simple acts of kindness and generosity, impressing on us their own thoughts and the words to be spoken. So you may find, for example, that while you stand at the bus stop on your way to work, you might suddenly feel compelled to speak to the person next to you, striking up a conversation and sharing the time of day. You might find yourself listening to a problem they wish to share, or that they have not spoken to another person for days and are simply grateful for the chance to chat. Similarly, the other world could inspire you to make a phone call to a friend or relative you haven't spoken to for months, or even years, at a time when they are in great need of support.

This happened to me a year or so ago. I was sitting at my desk working and suddenly had the strongest impulse to call an old school friend I hadn't spoken to in fifteen years. Nobody was home so I left a message, 'Hi, I'm just thinking about you. Try to call me back when you can.'

When my friend phoned back that evening, the first thing she said was, 'Why did you ring me today?'

'I've no idea,' I told her, 'I just felt I should.'

She then told me that when I called she was attending her grandfather's funeral. I'd met him many times when I was a child and knew she was incredibly close to him. On hearing this news I realised that the other world must have inspired me to call her. I'm sure many of you have had times when this kind of thing has happened, and for me it just goes to show that inspiration like this is indeed open to us all.

In a similar vein, while shopping in my local supermarket recently I noticed a middle-aged woman selecting a range of cheeses from the deli counter. As I wandered past her I felt an overwhelming need to speak to her. There was no revelation as such and I received no direct thoughts from the spirit world, but instead a strong sense that it was important to speak to her. Feeling like a stalker, and with no real thought in my mind as to why I needed to connect with her, I followed her around as she did her shopping, waiting for the right moment to make eye contact and strike up a conversation. Somewhere between the fresh bread and the cream cakes I managed to catch her glance, and as soon as I did her eyes filled with tears. 'Fancy seeing you here,' she said. 'I saw you last year at the Towngate Theatre in Basildon.'

I couldn't help feeling relieved that the conversation had started so easily – without me having to mention the weather or ask her the time – and before I could say a word in reply, she told me she was buying bread to make sandwiches for a funeral the next day. By this point she was quite emotional and I reached forward and took her hand. As soon as I did, I felt a strong presence from the other world.

'Your mother has passed, hasn't she?' I said gently.

The poor woman's mouth fell open. 'How did you know?'

I explained that I felt her mother next to me and she wanted to tell her daughter that she was fine now. I then heard the name Mary being called, and to my delight the woman confirmed that it was her mother's name.

Other information came through which I shared with the woman, who was by now shaking, with emotion and excitement. Before I left her I was enormously touched when she said, 'Thank you so much. I knew Mum would come through if she could. Now I'll be able to get through the funeral tomorrow, knowing that she's OK.'

I'm not one for doing spontaneous readings when going about my day-to-day business, but sometimes, when inspired, it just feels so right. As I pushed my trolley away and continued with my shopping, I felt a real sense of pride, not in myself but in those who work with me. It was incredibly fulfilling once again to receive evidence that when we are truly open to helping the spirit people and prepared to go out on a limb on their behalf, wonderful miracles can be performed.

So, if you are genuinely receptive in your own life to how the other world is able to inspire you, maybe from now on the question will not be what can the spirit world do for you, but rather what can you do for them. If you can demonstrate that you are prepared to serve – to work with the spirit people selflessly – then a relationship with them may be forged that will last a lifetime.

I'm sure that each of you will find your own unique ways in which you can begin to assist and serve the spirit world, but I believe the most important element of all is that we start by showing real integrity, kindness and devotion to one another. If we can do this, the same kindness and devotion will in turn be shown by the spirit people towards us. I've been asked many times why I am lucky enough to see and sense those who dwell within the other world, to which I answer that it has been my earnest desire over the past twenty-something years to allow them into my life and to walk this world with them at my side. I have never for a moment lost my absolute belief in their existence, which has been with me for as long as I can remember. I have grown up with them – they have seen me develop from boy to man – and there has never been a day when they have not watched over me. This is how I see it; they are my friends. So, all I can say to those of you who wish to see and embrace the angels for yourselves is invite them into your world and make them your friends.

10
A Lighter, Brighter You

'When I do good, I feel good; when I do bad, I feel bad. And that is my religion.'

Abraham Lincoln

It was daytime yet the heavy curtains in the room where I stood were still drawn, the only light coming from the early morning sunshine seeping in around the curtain edges. Peering around me, I could make out along one wall bookshelves housing a vast array of books and an impromptu bookend in the form of a large ceramic cat ornament. As my eyes became more accustomed to the gloom, I noticed that the bed in front of me did not appear to have been slept in, its old-fashioned candlewick bedspread neatly smoothed over the pillows. As far as I could see there was no one else in the room, yet I suddenly had the overwhelming feeling I was not alone. My heart lurched as I spun round, but no one was there. I moved further into the room, still peering through the dim light. Then I stopped in horror. On the floor at the other side of the bed, lay the body of an elderly woman, dressed in a pink nightdress and floral slippers, her long, grey hair straggled across her face.

The shock of seeing this woman was so great that it jolted me from sleep and I sat bolt upright with a gasp. Then I looked cautiously around me and was never more relieved to find myself in my own bed. I leaned back against the headboard, trying to pull myself together and thinking that what

I'd seen was so real it was as if I'd been in the room with this poor unfortunate woman. Finally convincing myself that it was nothing more than a bad dream, I sank back down onto the pillows, closed my eyes and once more drifted off to sleep.

I was busy the next day and thoughts of the dream left me, so the last thing I expected was to have the same dream that night, and indeed the one after that. Each time I saw a little more detail than before and came to feel that I knew the contents of the room by heart – the faded pink of the bedspread, the apple green lightshade hanging from the ceiling, the grain of the mahogany of the antique wardrobe, even the half-empty cup of tea that sat at the bedside. The dream seemed to go on for longer each time, but always ended with me gazing down in shock at this unknown woman on the floor.

I mentioned this experience to a friend who has an interest in the analysis of dreams, but he was quite perplexed as to what it could mean – and to be honest I had no idea either. I'm used to seeing and feeling the most bizarre things, but this recurring theme really had me confused.

During a meditation I asked the spirit world why I was having this dream, but whether I was blocking the answer or the spirit people were unable or unprepared to tell me, no explanation came. Yet I knew that I must have been seeing these things for a reason – one that was far more than coincidence and surely on some level orchestrated for a purpose. So trusting that all would eventually become clear, as I have learned to do time and again over the years, the next night I placed a notepad and pen at the side of my bed, ready to jot down on waking anything I witnessed during my sleep state.

Typically, things came to a head that very night, and as it turned out my notepad was superfluous to requirements. While asleep, I once again found myself looking around that oh-so-familiar bedroom and had a rare moment of clarity when, though I didn't wake up, I became aware that I was having a dream. It may seem strange but I remember thinking that maybe I could get to the bottom of this now. It's an odd feeling when you become aware that you're in a dream, because you can then take in so much more detail and investigate various aspects of what you are being shown.

Determined to see if I could at last find out who the unfortunate woman was, I walked directly to where I knew she would be lying, only to discover to my complete amazement that she wasn't there. Bizarrely, I then felt compelled to lie in the place where I had seen her. I had no idea why I was doing this and was finding it increasingly difficult to separate the dream from my imagination – I no longer knew whether this was a sleeping or waking experience.

Convincing myself that it was still only a dream and that I should just go with it, I lay down on the carpet and stayed there. Nothing more happened – it was just me lying there on my side, gazing at the pink swirly carpet for what felt like an age. It dawned on me at some point that the poor woman had done exactly this – she had lain on the floor in the same position for some time, until the final spark of life had ebbed from her body. No one came to find her and she was unable to move or speak, drifting in and out of consciousness until eventually her passing came.

There was no sudden jolt awake that night and I continued to sleep on until morning. I lay in bed, going over the experiences of the night in my mind and feeling even more confused than before. I was just about to reach for my notepad and pen when the telephone rang, making me jump out of my skin. I wondered who on earth could be calling so early, but a quick glance at the bedside clock informed me that it was past ten o'clock – very late even by my standards.

I picked up the phone to find a woman in floods of tears, apologising for calling on my home line and explaining as best she could that she'd been given my number by a friend of a friend. 'I'm so sorry,' she wept, 'but I couldn't think how else I could get to speak to you quickly.'

The distraught woman's name was Sharon and she explained that her mother had just died and she was desperate to hear from her. 'Please can you help?' she implored, 'I think it's all my fault.'

As I did my best to calm her down, the images from my dreams of the last few nights were flooding into my head with intensity and I couldn't help asking Sharon whether her mother had been found lying in her bedroom after she passed. My question was initially met with silence, then a small voice came back, 'How could you possibly know that?'

Even I had goosebumps as I asked Sharon whether her mother had long grey hair and was wearing a pink nightdress, having been found lying on the floor to the side of her bed. When the stunned response came that this was correct, I agreed there and then to see Sharon that same day. Just as she was desperate to hear from her late mother, I was anxious to find out what my recurring dream was all about, and was more than happy to forego my lunch break if it meant my nights might be my own again.

When the doorbell rang at my studio later, I went down the stairs and opened the door to find a woman in her late forties looking back at me. I'm sure she would usually have been meticulous in her appearance, but her eyes were now red and puffy from crying and she hadn't troubled with any make-up, perhaps knowing there would be more tears to come – indeed they started to flow again as soon as she set eyes on me. I sat her on the comfy sofa in the corner of my studio and we chatted for a while to break the ice. I went on to explain the strange dreams I'd been having for the past few nights. Sharon listened open mouthed and gasped aloud when I mentioned the ceramic cat ornament. 'That's it, that's my mum's room!' she exclaimed.

I proceeded to try and make a link to the spirit world on Sharon's behalf and was greatly relieved when her mother appeared. Strangely enough this was the first time I felt I knew anything about her, since previously I'd only seen her as if in a vision. I started to describe her but then found myself lost for words because I was experiencing a strange sensation. As Sharon's mother stood by me I became increasingly aware that she was not exactly a sweet elderly lady full of love and tenderness for her bereft daughter; in fact she seemed quite the opposite.

It seemed almost impossible that I should be faced with the prospect of saying to a grieving daughter, 'Your mother is here and she gives me the strongest impression that she was an incredibly difficult woman while she was alive. I know that she disliked her neighbours intensely and was forever falling out with her family and friends over the slightest little thing.' But what else could I do? If it was a statement I believed to be evidential, I had to pass it on, albeit with as much sensitivity as I could muster.

As I started to explain all this to Sharon, she became less emotional, drying her eyes and sitting with her hands firmly clasped in her lap, agreeing wholeheartedly with everything I was relating.

'She gives me the name Pearl,' I said.

Sharon rolled her eyes. 'That's right – or that's what she made us call her anyway. She'd never let us say Mum, it always had to be Pearl, even though her real name was Vera. But she'd kill me if she knew I'd told you that.'

There was something about the way Sharon said this that made us both laugh, and it was good to lighten the mood a little as I carried on with the reading.

'Pearl is showing me that she had more than one husband,' I informed Sharon next.

'That's putting it mildly,' she replied with a smile. 'She was married three times. They all died before her – we used to wonder whether she'd bumped them all off.'

We laughed again, but I became a little confused by the information that then came through. It was rather like listening to stereo speakers, with different sounds coming from each at the same time. On the one hand I was receiving that Pearl had been the mother of seven children, and on the other I had the overwhelming impression that Sharon was the only child.

'There were seven of us altogether from the various marriages,' Sharon clarified. 'But I was the only one who kept in touch with Pearl – the others couldn't be bothered.'

On hearing this, I felt guided to say now that Pearl was in the other world she wanted to send her love to all her children. Sharon almost grunted in disbelief. 'It's a bit late for that,' she said. 'They won't want to know.'

This made me wonder whether I'd got my wires crossed because it seemed clear that messages of love were the last thing Sharon expected from the mother she had known. I therefore endeavoured to give whatever evidential statements I could to prove that this was indeed Sharon's mother communicating with me.

As soon as I asked for facts to be given, a barrage of information flooded my mind. I described how Pearl had poisoned her neighbour's cat because it repeatedly messed in her garden; how she had been cautioned by the police for verbal abuse aimed at other neighbours; and how she would insist on having a nip of brandy each evening before she retired, 'for medicinal purposes only' of course.

All these facts were confirmed by Sharon, who then added that she had been so appalled about the cat that she hadn't spoken to her mother for several weeks after the incident. As I knew that, however difficult she might have been in life, this was indeed Pearl who was coming through, I felt a little more confident to express exactly what it was she wished to say.

Pearl then gave me a strong impression of her and her daughter arguing in the days before she passed. I understood that Sharon would normally pop round from her nearby home each night to make sure that Pearl, who was in ailing health, had got herself to bed safely. But Sharon was so upset after the row that she didn't go round again, and so had left her mother for four nights before she eventually calmed down sufficiently to check up on her – and this was when she discovered she had passed.

'I know she was a very hard woman,' Sharon told me, becoming emotional again, 'but I can never forgive myself. She must have fallen and was lying there on her own, waiting for me to go round – and I wasn't there for her.'

No sooner had the words left Sharon's mouth than her mother's response came: 'It doesn't matter now, darlin'. I love you. I always did – I could just never say it or show it.'

On hearing this, Sharon asked doubtfully, 'How could she possibly forgive me?'

I could only repeat what I was receiving from Pearl, that she was a changed woman, a better person in the other world. She was now free from physical pain, the anger and grief at having lost husband after husband and the trauma of falling out with her children one by one – all the things that had made her a very bitter and unhappy woman in this lifetime had now fallen away. From her vantage point in the other world, she could see things far more clearly than she had for many years.

Once more, tears streamed down Sharon's face. I told her that Pearl wanted all her children at her funeral, and more than that was hoping Sharon would speak on her behalf. 'She's asking that you tell them all you have come here today and that she's sorry for being such a nuisance.' I paused, sensing Pearl was feeling quite awkward about the next thing she wanted to say, but as soon as I understood, I passed her wishes on to Sharon. 'Your mother is also saying that, if you feel able, from this point onwards she would like you to refer to her as Mum and not Pearl.'

The last impression I had from Pearl was that she wanted me to tell her daughter, 'Let's forgive each other, let's move on. It's not too late to be mother and daughter.'

Sharon and I chatted for a little while after the reading and I think she really needed to share with me some of the things she had gone through with Pearl. It felt like some sort of therapy for her, despite my complete lack of qualifications in that regard; she needed to purge herself and perhaps try to justify why she hadn't gone back to visit her mum after the row. But she could see that her mother now recognised she'd had very little time to listen to any problems Sharon may have had, or to give her emotional support when she needed it. Sharon said she had only ever wanted her mum to get to know her, but eventually had to give up. I then felt Pearl's presence again and passed on her message. 'You can speak to me now. From here, I can be the mother you wanted me to be; the mother I always wanted to be, but never knew how.'

I'm delighted to say that Sharon walked out of the room a different woman – all smiles and her head held high. I like to think that this contact from her mother, showing herself from an entirely new perspective, helped Sharon to deal with what had happened and to move on.

Looking back now, I find it fascinating that Pearl had been so determined to get a message through to her daughter that she had been influencing me in my sleep state, with strong imagery and impressions, showing me how she had passed and allowing me to see her at the end of her life.

I also found it intriguing that Sharon had somehow come across my home phone number from 'a friend of a friend', and I wondered just what might have been going on behind the scenes in the spirit world to orchestrate this. The more I pondered, the more wonderful it seemed that the other world knew I would read for Pearl's daughter long before I did. Perhaps they influenced her in some way, ultimately facilitating their communication with her.

I guess many of us have relationships and friendships with people who have at some point in their lives demonstrated difficult behaviour. Perhaps through illness or traumatic life experiences they changed from the person we loved into someone full of angst, anger and negativity. Or it could be that their life path took them in such a different direction from our own that we no longer related to them as we once did. As we grow and progress, our desires, needs and aspirations change, along with our views on many different subjects, so it's not unusual to find we no longer have the same affinity with people we related to in the past. This brings to mind the old saying that people come into your life 'for a reason, a season or a lifetime'.

If you have fallen out with, or spoken harsh words to a loved one before they passed to the other world, without the opportunity to apologise or resolve what happened, you may understandably find yourself full of remorse and regret. But we should try to remember that, free from the body, the spirit within each of us can express itself as it truly is. Those who pass to the other world will in time regain an even temperament, recognising, just as you do, that certain things should never have been said or done. They will want to rectify things, apologise and seek closure as much as you will. So don't ever think all hope is lost – speak to them in your mind, deal with the issues between you honestly and frankly and try to let the pain go. Physical death never severs a relationship – it will continue to exist and evolve wherever you find yourselves, either in this world or the next.

I'm sure we have all at some point or another fallen out with a loved one or valued friend, often over the most incidental thing. It's so easy to allow these episodes to be blown out of all proportion and quickly find ourselves at war with the very people we're supposed to love and cherish. If you recognise this situation for yourself, try to rectify it now – not tomorrow or next week, but today. Your attempt at reconciliation may be rebuffed, your apology ignored or your embrace rejected, but at least you tried and will know in your heart that you could have done no more.

On the other hand, your attempt at resolution may be welcomed with open arms and what could have been a lifetime of disconnection avoided. The power lies in your endeavour to resolve, heal and turn a negative situation around for good. Don't wait until someone passes to the other world before you try to make amends – do it at once and learn to forgive them and yourself in the process. The more we try to keep our life positive the more pleasurable our journey through it will be. I certainly don't profess to be perfect and I have definitely made mistakes in the past with my friends and family, but it is important that we recognise where we have gone wrong and strive to mend the bridges that have been broken in the process. And if any of us feel we lack the courage to rectify difficult issues on our own, we have only to remember that our spirit friends and angel companions are there to be called upon, ever willing to inspire and support us in the hope of bringing a lasting sense of peace and contentment.

For all of us, while we're here experiencing this life on Earth, it is necessary to accept change, because the world we inhabit is itself in a continuous state of flux. We have only to look out of our windows to see day turning into night, night into day and the ever-changing nature of the seasons. Just as surely, with each passing day, many are born into our world and many pass into the next. Learning to accept this can be hugely liberating; by reminding ourselves that we are here in this world for such a short time in the overall scheme of things, we free ourselves to move on. Holding on to past regrets, looking back at what might have been, allowing ourselves to become trapped in our yesterdays are all things that will deter us from becoming all we can be. Progression of the soul is an eternal process and we should never feel it's too late to seize the day and make changes within our lives. We are here on earth to experience everything a physical life can offer, in all its wondrous glory, but this is only a small part of our existence and there will be unlimited additional chances for your spirit to shine. Rather than wasting time and energy thinking about what you cannot change, look at each day as a new chance to create a better present and future for you and those you love.

I once read an article that explained how important it is to release ourselves from certain past pledges and promises. The gist was that from the day we're born, right through our lives, promises are made on many levels – the promise of enduring love to a partner, the vows we make during a wedding ceremony, promises to our closest friends always to be there to support them, or the pledges we might undertake as we join different societies or groups. At the time of making these declarations we truly mean them, but I'm sure we all recognise that, even with the best of intentions, circumstances change and things may no longer hold the same relevance they once did. We are often faced with difficult decisions and there are times in our lives when we need to distance ourselves from certain people or situations, recognising what limits us and moving on from that which no longer makes us happy. Yet because we constantly make declarations that can have a powerful effect on the way we live, or feel we ought to live, it's easy to see how we might become weighed down. It could therefore be very beneficial if, as a part of our spiritual housekeeping process, we learn to release ourselves from any promises made in the past that are no longer relevant to our current lives.

I have thought about this particular concept on many occasions and from time to time use it when working with clients, either in one-to-one readings or healing sessions. I sometimes offer a particular affirmation that my client might like to try, such as, 'I free myself from any past promises and pledges that bear no relevance to my life at this time.' If they feel comfortable in doing so, I ask them to repeat this affirmation in a positive and joyous way so that it might help them enter into a new, positive way of being.

An example might be a woman who promised herself to her husband in a religious service, committing herself to this promise with every fibre of her being, but who has found herself by choice single years later. She may then wish to start a new relationship after her failed marriage, but is finding it difficult to move on successfully because something in her unconscious mind is holding onto the previous commitment. By speaking the affirmation, she might consciously release herself from the deep-rooted obligation.

You might wish to try this for yourself, especially if you feel your life is not moving on or evolving in the way you would like. A close friend of mine, who is an enthusiastic devotee of the singer Madonna, once told me that a key ingredient of why she still holds such a fascination is her ongoing ability to change the style of her music, her look and the messages she conveys in her song lyrics and live performances. Her ethos is one of always moving forward, absorbing and experimenting with the latest trends and styles, and never looking back or repeating herself, no matter how successful it may have been at the time. I completely agree, but would also say there is no reason why such a practice should be confined to those in the public eye – it is open to every one of us. Life dictates that we shouldn't stand still for too long, so I guess if you've worn beige all your life you could try going a little crazy tomorrow and choose orange! It's about not feeling the need to conform every step of the way – we are born to be individuals, to express ourselves in our own unique and positive way.

In my view this is the essence of life. Whether we realise it or not, each of us is on a journey of self-discovery and it is my great belief that our spirit friends, guides and those in the angelic realm want to see us express all the wonder that is naturally within us – while we're still here, alive in this world. So let's not wait – as Sharon's mother Pearl did – until we return home to the spirit world before we learn to sing our song and dance our dance.

One of my favourite films is *Shirley Valentine*. Our Shirley, much in need of a change of scene, tries to persuade her husband to go on holiday with her. After his adamant declaration that he's 'going to no Greece', she takes off anyway with a friend, who deserts her soon after arriving. Shirley finds herself spending time on her own, possibly for the first time in her life. There is no one else to worry about for a couple of weeks – she doesn't have to be a wife, mother or daughter, but can focus on just being Shirley, and it's fascinating to follow her journey of self-discovery as she does so.

I'm not suggesting that we should all pack our bags and leave the country, but I think what the film tells us so clearly is that there are moments when each of us, just for a change, should take a deep breath and really think about ourselves. This could simply mean spending an hour in the park, a day by the shore, or any other little chunks of time when the world will continue happily without our input. I know sometimes we all get stuck in a routine and it feels as though we are simply existing rather than truly living. So allow me to suggest that we should all have our 'Shirley Valentine moment', stepping outside our comfort zone to stand tall and shine. You may also find that inviting spirit into your life will give you the courage and strength to be anything you want to be and live this life to the full.

Moments of quiet reflection are crucial for the spiritual enquirer – someone who is open enough to look beyond this world and embrace an understanding that we will one day pass on to the next. Brief intervals of solitude, with no inter-ruptions from the hurly-burly of modern-day living, help us appreciate just who we are, what we want from life and what we feel we can give in this lifetime – as well as providing opportunities for our spirit friends to walk with us. However busy we are, with a little bit of forethought most of us can set aside some 'me time' and learn to appreciate that we can be materially secure and happy in our home lives while at the same time living a very spiritual existence – we do not have to run off to a monastery to achieve this! Living spiritually is more about embracing all that life gives to us and what we can give back – smiling at a stranger, lending a helping hand where we can and being mindful that we are part of a loving universe. We are all connected and symbiotic, so by helping others we are in essence lifting ourselves higher and aiding spiritual happiness and progression for everyone.

For us to reach a place in our lives where we can begin to progress, we may first of all need consciously to forgive ourselves for anything negative we have been responsible for in the past. With this in mind, I would suggest that you choose to consider the following affirmation: 'I forgive myself for all past negative action, word and thought, so that I may move forward in love.' As with all affirmations, it is important to repeat a number of times, just as it is to believe absolutely in the meaning of the words as we speak them. If you are not inclined to verbal affirmations, why not write down the words on a piece of paper and stick it on your fridge door – then each time you see it throughout the day you will be consolidating the intention behind the words, bringing the message to the forefront of your mind.

Beyond affirmation, another useful tool to help us along the path towards transformation is that of visualisation. As simple as it sounds, seeing ourselves in our mind's eye as changed and improved can have a massively positive effect. I've worked with many people over the years who have a very poor self image, much of which has been created from early traumatic experiences or their peer group or even family telling them that they are silly, stupid, dumpy, unattractive and so on. Something only has to be said enough times for us to start to believe it. So if you feel this resonates with you, I would suggest you take time out to close your eyes and imagine yourself as you are now – take a good, long look and then cast aside that image. Next, see yourself walking tall, smiling and proud of who you are. Even though you may think you are a million miles removed from, say, a confident, glamorous movie star, simply visualise and recognise yourself as the wonderful, vibrant, unique person you are. You might be surprised to find the beauty that comes from within will express itself outwardly and dazzle those around you.

Not so long ago, as I walked down the High Street in the town where I live, the weather grey and drizzly, I was struck by the expressions on the faces of the people passing by – they looked so miserable as they went about their daily business. I tried to put an optimistic slant on things by simply blaming the weather and made my way towards the local stationer.

A little way ahead of me, in stark contrast to the mood on the street, I heard the sound of raucous laughter. As I drew nearer I saw it was coming from a young woman in her mid-twenties sitting in a wheelchair. I'd seen her around several times before, occasionally exchanging a few words but never really engaging in a proper conversation. She carried on laughing as her mother knelt down at her side, also laughing. It was so infectious I couldn't help smiling myself. I made a quip about what they were finding so funny, and the mother turned to me and said, 'Nothing in particular, we're always like this – we keep setting each other off.'

We chatted for a few minutes, during which I learned that the woman's daughter, Emily, suffered from cerebral palsy. I noticed what a beautiful girl she was, and her ever-present smile and lively dancing eyes. There was something very special about her, not only her happy disposition but the caring, loving soul I could sense within – and this was despite having to contend with physical problems most people never have to face. She and her mum had clearly learned something most of us hadn't – and that was simply to laugh hard on a dull, dreary day and make the most of every little opportunity that came their way.

After a few moments of swapping pleasantries, Emily's mother observed, 'It's amazing how many people come up to us in the street and just start chatting. We both love it, but the only thing that gets on Emily's nerves is when people talk to me about her, rather than talking directly to her.'

At that point, of course, I realised I was similarly at fault, so I made a face to show I knew I was guilty as charged and then smiled sheepishly. 'So, as I was about to say,' I began with a wink, looking directly at her this time.

She giggled and waved a hand dismissively. 'It's OK,' she said, 'I'll let you off.'

'But I really did want to say,' I continued, 'you have a smile that could light up a whole street – and lord knows this one needs it.'

We spoke at length, putting the world to rights and swapping thoughts about how we could try to raise a smile from the passers-by. Although what Emily said took a little time, she was a very bright and witty young woman and I felt truly chastened that I might initially have assumed otherwise. It was a stark reminder of the need to look beyond a person's physical appearance and take the time to communicate properly – who knows what offence we could unwittingly cause or what we ourselves might miss out on when we fail to do so. It also hit home to me just how much more approachable we make ourselves when we smile.

I often wonder how many of us at times feel a little lonely and perhaps want to converse with the people around us, but are held back from reaching out and making new friends by a lack of confidence or fear of rejection. It costs so little to make contact in the simplest of ways, which then often reaps the reward of a warm response, as though the other person is only too pleased the ice has been broken. They might be a complete stranger or someone you see every day when out walking but have never wanted to intrude on their space. It doesn't matter, just be prepared to give it a try – give yourself the chance to give them a chance. You may spend only a few pleasant moments together, but you never know, this little interlude might lead to a lasting friendship.

As for Emily, I really did feel she had a magnetic quality about her. Her mother's reference to people stopping them wherever they went made me wonder if they were on an unconscious level sensing her willingness to share with them. As I said goodbye, Emily's mum's parting comment was, 'Do you know, she's got so many friends it's amazing.' Then she grinned at me and added, 'You're in trouble yourself now – you'll have to stop and chat every time we see you.'

'It will be my pleasure,' I told her, and as I moved on I couldn't help but reflect on how incredibly rewarding it was that, just by stopping for a few moments, I now had two new friends. But maybe it wasn't really so incredible after all – it might just be that Emily has simply mastered the art of smiling more and letting more people in.

If I think about our friends in the other world, I find it inconceivable that two spirit beings might walk past each other without warmly acknowledging the other's presence. I suppose one of the reasons things are so different in our world is that we have a tendency to be self-absorbed or self-conscious, and I'm sure that this has a huge effect on our willingness to participate and become part of a group or a true member of society. We should also bear in mind that so often when we first meet someone we feel is not responding to us particularly warmly, we naturally assume it's because of something they don't like about us, whereas the real reason someone might seem stand-offish, unfriendly or even a little rude frequently turns out to be attributable to their own fears and insecurities.

Thinking about this reminds me of a neighbour who lived downstairs from me but wouldn't even acknowledge me when our paths crossed on the stairwell. It was only after I knocked on her door with a letter that had been incorrectly delivered to me, and tried to strike up a conversation with her, that I learned she was just incredibly shy. But after our first proper conversation we struck up quite a friendship.

I can't imagine such insecurities exist in the spirit world – it would be a very bizarre state of affairs if our guides were unable to commune with us because they were suffering from debilitating shyness or even a fear that we might not like them! So at the risk of sounding like a hopeless fantasist again, could we not all try to cast aside our insecurities and just smile, chat and laugh with our fellow companions here in this world; the sound of our happiness may have a hugely beneficial effect on somebody's otherwise dull and grey day. I'm again reminded at this point of the words of Marianne Williamson I quoted in Chapter 3: '. . . as we let our own light shine, we unconsciously give other people permission to do the same. As we are liberated from our fear, our presence automatically liberates others.' We are currently having this physical experience on Earth for a reason and it should be embraced and enjoyed; what better way to achieve this than to share our journey positively and enthusiastically with those around us?

From time to time something happens in our world that shocks us all to the core, and this is never more apparent than in the case of a large-scale natural disaster. At the time of writing this chapter, the news is consumed by reports of the terrible scenes following the catastrophic earthquake in Haiti. There can't be a person in the world with access to a television, radio or the internet who isn't aware of the tens if not hundreds of thousands of people who have lost their lives in this disaster. Imprinted in our minds are images of homes reduced to rubble, hungry children walking alone through dusty, destroyed streets and survivors mourning their dead, while at the same time despairing that the aid they have been promised is not getting through to them. I can only hope this latter problem will be swiftly resolved – our government has pledged a considerable sum of money to help this stricken land and I hear the general public have donated even more. Firefighters and rescue workers from Britain have flown out to assist, and just this morning I heard of the rescue of a sixteen-month-old girl who had been trapped alone for days, calling out for someone to come to her aid.

As I think about these events my mind naturally goes to how those in the spirit world view such catastrophes and how they might try to intervene at times like this. While watching a news item a couple of days ago, the reporter indicated where Haiti appeared on the world map. Somehow seeing the exact location highlighted like this triggered something in my mind and I felt an overwhelming need to close my eyes and concentrate on that region. I visualised the globe first, then focused my attention on Haiti in the hope that I might learn something of how the spirit world viewed this country and what they might be trying to do to assist the people there.

Within a second, imagery and thought flooded my mind and I immediately became aware of Zintar by my side. He was able to give me clear images, not of the physical destruction but rather, I believe, of how he himself was viewing this place. To begin with I saw only dazzling white light, but then I could pick out the vague outlines of ruined buildings as well as some of the people. The striking thing about this vision was that I was not seeing these people physically but spiritually. What I mean by this is that it felt as though I were looking at their spirit bodies rather than their physical bodies – they were still very much alive in this world, but I was somehow able to see beyond their worn-out and battered appearance and view through Zintar's eyes how they would appear to him.

At first I questioned what I was seeing, but then Zintar's thoughts came clearly into my mind. 'We are doing all that we can. We may best serve our brothers and sisters in this land first by healing their souls, in the hope that this healing will then spread into their emotional, mental and physical bodies.'

I was completely bowled over by this revelation. To me it made perfect sense that the spirit people would heal our spirit bodies first and foremost so that this energy might then have a positive effect on all our other aspects.

Zintar's thoughts continued in my mind. 'We ask that those in your world physically feed them, address their bodily wounds and keep them safe. We in the other world will endeavour to change the atmosphere of this place from negative into positive energy and try to wipe away the fearful and angry emotions that have been created because of the disaster. We hope there will be a brighter tomorrow and a new beginning for those who live there.'

As these thoughts blended with my own, I opened my eyes to look once more at the news footage on the television. I wondered at this point why I had seen Haiti itself bathed in white light, where this light had come from and what its purpose was; and then once again, quick as a flash, I received thoughts from Zintar. The light, he impressed on me, was manifested by the source of all creation, the energy that surrounds us continuously, which was now being concentrated over the land of Haiti by the prayers, thoughts and good intentions of millions of people in our world – together with the infinite number of minds in the other world, all focusing on this one place in the hope that healing and peace would be sent there.

This fascinating revelation took my mind back to my thoughts on the importance of community and being part of a group; when many people focus their thoughts and attention on an individual, place or situation, sometimes immensely positive changes will manifest as a result.

A good friend of mine once introduced me to a small charity set up to sponsor young Buddhist monks in exile from Tibet and now living in northern India. The charity was looking for people in the West who might be in a position to fund individual monks throughout their studies in Buddhism. After speaking with my friend, I felt compelled to contact the charity and sponsor a monk myself, as a result of which he and I have been exchanging correspondence ever since – a discourse I have greatly enjoyed.

A few years after I became a sponsor, I bumped into my friend again and she told me an extraordinary story. Some months previously, she had written to the monk she sponsors and confided to him that she had been diagnosed with cancer. The doctors had led her to believe the outlook was not favourable, and she shared in the letter her worries and concerns.

Several weeks later, my friend was amazed to be told that her cancer had begun to shrink and there was suddenly now real hope of a good outcome. Then she received a letter from her monk, who told her as soon as he'd heard of her plight he enlisted the help of all the other monks in his monastery and together they had regularly chanted and prayed that she might be healed.

As she related this story, my friend talked of her absolute belief that she had received such positive results as a direct consequence of these wonderful people, thousands of miles away, focusing on her and her wellbeing. I would be hard pushed to think of a more powerful justification for my belief in the power of positive thought, not least when that thought is shared by the many rather than the few.

We need only look back through our history books or revisit old tales and fables to appreciate how many people before us have sought the meaning of life. Men and women have for centuries gone on pilgrimages throughout the world, to places such as Lourdes, Mecca, Bodhgaya and Varanasi, each hoping to achieve a closer connection with their god. I would suggest that, whether we know it or not, this desire to reach higher is innate within every single one of us.

I'm sure that many people travel to sacred places in search of spiritual enlightenment because they feel there will be a heightened atmosphere or powerful energy existing there – and that this energy has been enhanced by the genuine devotion of the many thousands of men, women and children who have visited these places over the years. They go hoping for an epiphany, to unlock something amazing from within, to stimulate a connection that will lend further insight into the meaning of life.

I fully understand why people make such pilgrimages, and while each individual is free to follow whichever path they choose, I am personally drawn to another option. I once heard someone say that we are all travellers in life but the only journey ever truly worth taking is the journey within. Needless to say, this is a sentiment I wholeheartedly agree with; by looking inward, recognising and connecting with the divine spark within, you will also connect with the creative force of the universe, of which we are all a part.

With this in mind, might we not also consider that spiritual realisation can be achieved far closer to home? I believe all the answers we could ever need lie already within us, in that part of us that is everlasting, our own spirit self. Has it not been said many times before, by religious scholars, that the kingdom of heaven lies within?

Our angel friends in the other world have no doubt discovered this for themselves, achieving through trial and tribulation the state of understanding that has elevated them into the sphere they now inhabit. From their vantage point in the other world they watch over us, walking with us through-out our lives – there to console, inspire and love us during the time we spend here on this Earth. So try never to doubt their ability to intercede at times on our behalf, to allow us to see and appreciate all the blessings that surround us. Remember always that we are loved, that our lives are infinitely precious and that we should value every moment we spend here; for it is a moment in which we have the potential to grow, and in so doing become closer to the truth.

Wherever you are on your journey through life, I hope you will take away with you from this book the thought that so much is possible for you. Recognise that the only limitations we have are those we place on ourselves. Know that you are never alone and that the spirits and angels are here to walk this path with you. Be grateful and appreciative of all they do for you, and in turn remember to thank them for the blessings they bring into your lives.

So go on, make them proud!